MAKING LOGO WORK

A Guide for Teachers

Janet Ainley and Ronnie Goldstein

Basil Blackwell

Acknowledgements

We would like to acknowledge a number of people who have helped in various ways to make it possible for this book to be completed. First and foremost, our thanks go to Peter Hastings and the staff of The Trinity School for welcoming us, and allowing us to work with their pupils. Our thanks also go to our colleagues in the Science Education Department at Warwick University. Their cooperation made it possible for us to have time to work in school and to write this book, and discussions with them have helped to clarify our thoughts on many occasions. Other friends have helped us by sharing their experiences of using Logo; in particular, Marilyn Metz, Chris Evans and staff at Marlborough School, and the members of the ATM Logo working group.

Our greatest thanks, however, go to the children and some of our students, who have allowed us to use their work.

© Janet Ainley and Ronnie Goldstein 1988

First published 1988

Published by Basil Blackwell Ltd
108 Cowley Road
Oxford OX4 1JF
England

British Library Cataloguing in Publication Data

Ainley, Janet
   Making Logo work: a guide for teachers.
   1. Education—Data processing   2. LOGO
   (Computer program language)
   I. Title   II. Goldstein, Ronnie
   370'.28'5404   LB1028.43

ISBN 0–631–15703–4

Typeset in 10/11½ Ehrhardt
by Opus, Oxford
Printed in Hong Kong by Wing King Tong Co. Ltd.

Contents

Introduction

When we were planning this book, we put in a chapter entitled 'Why Logo?', in which we tried to explain our reasons for wanting Logo in our classrooms. This turned out to be not one question, but many. Why use Logo rather than other programming languages? Why have computers in mathematics classrooms? Why use Logo to let children work on their own projects? Why is programming a valuable activity for children?

A short, but rather evasive, answer to all these questions would be 'because Logo fits so well into the way we want to teach, and the way we want children to learn'. A longer answer turned out, in a way, to be the rest of this book, although it would be unrealistic to hope that we have answered every possible aspect of the question. What we have tried to do is to describe our own experiences teaching Logo and the kind of work that children in our classes have done. Since Logo became available on microcomputers, many teachers and researchers have explored what children can do and learn, but generally this has only been done with small groups of children, or over short periods of time, and often away from the normal classroom setting. We began working with Logo in school because we wanted to find out what children would be able to do when they used Logo as part of their normal curriculum over an extended period of time.

It would not be appropriate to begin a book about the educational ideas associated with Logo without mentioning Seymour Papert, whose book *Mindstorms — Children, Computers and Powerful Ideas*[1] has prompted teachers to think about how Logo can open up new ways of teaching and learning. He designed Logo to be a language for learning so that children could take responsibility for what and how they learn. Many Logo enthusiasts may seem to be claiming that Logo is a revolutionary panacea which will solve all the problems of mathematics teaching. Despite our enthusiasm, this is not how we see Logo. We have tried to write about what Logo has to offer but also to be realistic about the problems which may arise. Much of this is based on our experience of teaching Logo and, to put this into context, we would like to introduce you to the school where this took place.

The Trinity School

The Trinity School is a comprehensive school in Leamington Spa, Warwickshire, where Logo is used extensively in the mathematics department as well as in the computing department. The school has a progressive educational philosophy and, as it is part of the TVEI scheme, it also has plenty of computers. This rare combination of assets allows Logo to flourish.

There is a relaxed and friendly atmosphere in the school. The children do not wear uniforms, and all children and staff are called by their first names. It is very unusual to hear a teacher shouting at a child; the relationships between teachers and children are natural ones, and the children are given a lot of respect. This breeds confidence amongst the children, who are not afraid to say what they think.

Trinity is a Catholic school. Religion and theology are important, but there are no figurines or paintings on the walls to advertise religion. It would be contrary to the principles of the school to force children to worship, and so the termly masses are voluntary. Many of the children will attend, especially the Christmas Mass, which develops into a dance after an hour or so.

We have both taught in the mathematics department, which is at present equipped with two computers in each of the six mathematics rooms. The children work in twos and threes, and the environment which is described in Chapter 1 of this book is based on what the teachers at The Trinity School are trying to create. All the children we refer to by name in this book are from the school, and the work we describe is theirs. They were mostly 11 and 12 years old at the time, and the eight computers which the department then owned were networked and kept in one room.

None of this book would have been possible without the cooperation of many of the children and staff at The Trinity School, but the following children deserve our special thanks. They are responsible for most of the work we have described. In the text we have used pseudonyms.

Nik Barker	Luella Bartley
Sean Beattie	Lucy Benger
Charlotte Blunsom	David Bradshaw
Myles Cadden	Simon Cardinale
Adam Clark	Rupert Colbourne
Claire Connolly	Anne-Marie Corr
Rory Crone	Nic Devlin
Anne-Marie Duffy	Katie Dwyer
Adrian Dyde	Ben Farrell
Catherine Fleetwood	Hannah Gash
Helen Geddes	David Gee
Carlo Giorgio	Rachel Hart
Annette Lamb	Simon Lamb

Abigail Myers   Lucie Palmer
Ruth Partridge   Stephen Pennells
Claire Tuohy   Alex Vaquiero
Lucy Watts   Andy Whately
Katherine Wier

Versions of Logo

This is not a technical book, but it is about the use of some fairly new technology, and so it is inevitable that there will be technical references occasionally. Most versions of Logo fall into one of three categories. The American standard versions are LCSI (Logo Computer Systems Incorporated) and MIT (Massachusetts Institute of Technology). In this country, RML (Research Machines Ltd.) has its own standard, but although the Nimbus is made by RML, its version of Logo is a cross between the original RML Logo and LCSI Logo. In this book, when a feature which is being discussed depends on the version of Logo which is running, then we will refer to LCSI, MIT and RML, and RML Logo will be assumed to mean the original version for the 380Z and 480Z machines. Some of the more popular versions of Logo in British schools are listed here.

Logo	Category
Amstrad	LCSI
Apple	LCSI and MIT
Atari	LCSI
BBC Acornsoft	LCSI (with extensions)
BBC Logotron	LCSI
BBC Open Logo	
Commodore 64	MIT
RML 380Z	RML
RML 480Z	RML
RML Nimbus	RML–LCSI
Sinclair Spectrum	LCSI

This book contains a small amount of computer code, and this has all been written in Logotron Logo for the BBC machine. You are most unlikely to want to type any of this code into a computer. If you did, however, and you were using LCSI Logo, you would have no problems. With MIT Logo you would need to make one or two small changes. If you use an RML computer, many of the commands will be different. There are some profound differences between the three dialects of the Logo language, but for most children (and most teachers) these are not important. It will certainly not make any difference to whatever you might gain from reading this book if the machine you use does not run LCSI Logo.

1 Setting the Scene

In this opening chapter, we will describe the atmosphere and some of the Logo work at Bridgeton School. Bridgeton is not a real school, but it is not totally fanciful either. It is a school with many computers and, although this is certainly not yet typical, there are a few schools which have machines in many of the classrooms. All the Logo work we will describe at Bridgeton is based on that of our own classrooms or those of our colleagues. We have compiled scenes from many different sources because we believe that, working with Logo, the same educational philosophy can apply to all children. Bridgeton is intended to be a state school, but the children's ages range between 5 and 18 years. We hope that you will be prepared to suspend your disbelief in this respect.

Every classroom at Bridgeton School has a few machines, but they are scattered about and they do not dominate (Fig. 1.1). The work being done on the computers is very diverse. It covers many aspects of the curriculum and children of various ages are involved. There are plenty of other activities going on which do not require computers, and there are even one or two machines which are not being used at all. The children are all busy, and the atmosphere is like that of a good primary school, even though many of the children are older.

What are the computers being used for? One or two groups of children have chosen to practice a particular skill, or to solve a well-defined problem, and they are using short programs, but much of the software consists of larger, more-flexible packages. Many children are using word processors or databases, and others are achieving various effects with the help of a programming language such as Logo.

Bridgeton School has a reputation in the locality for its child-centred approach to education, and there are often

FIGURE 1.1 A classroom at Bridgeton School

visitors looking around. Mike is a teacher from another school in a different part of the town. The intakes of the two schools are similar, but the educational philosophies are very different. Mike is thinking of introducing Logo in his school, and he particularly wants to see the sort of work which his pupils may eventually be doing. The senior member of staff at Bridgeton who met him has suggested that he would learn a lot by visiting some classrooms on his own.

Mike walks up the stairs and along the corridor. When he arrives at the first classroom he is still rather apprehensive, and he knocks at the door even though it is open. At first no-one answers but, when he knocks again, one of the children nearby stands up and invites him to come in. The child looks about 10 or 11 years old, but she is clearly very confident.

'Isn't there a teacher in the room?' Mike asks.

'Yes, I'll take you to her', the child replies.

The teacher is sitting at a table in the middle of the room with a group of children, and Mike had not noticed her straight away. She offers him a welcoming smile and, without ever losing the contact she has with the small group where she is sitting, invites him to talk to the children.

Mike responds by going to the computer where Logo is being used. Annabel and Leena have drawn a cartoon character on the screen. He tries to join them unobtrusively, but they immediately stop what they are doing and start to describe their project.

'This is Dusty Bin. He's from a TV program, and his bow-tie spins... . Would you like to see?'

Mike nods his head, and the girls clear the screen and type the name of their procedure, DUSTY. The character itself is quickly drawn, but it takes a little longer for the tie to spin, as the turtle repeatedly draws it and rubs it out, each time in a different orientation (Fig. 1.2). When the tie stops spinning, the arms begin to revolve, and then the program ends.

'We've just got to make the legs move up and down, and we've finished.'

Annabel and Leena are very keen to talk about their project. They explain exactly how it all works, and it becomes clear that the most difficult phase of the project was a week or so ago. They had had many struggles to make the tie spin, but now they are consolidating those ideas, and the project is coming to a natural end.

'We've been working on Dusty Bin for a long time. We started just after half-term, but we want to finish it before Christmas.'

'What will you do next term?'

'I don't know really, but I'm sure we'll think of something.'

In the next classroom that Mike visits, the children are younger. Logo is running on all three computers, and there is also a group of children who are playing turtle games without a machine. They have arranged some chairs to form a sort of maze, and they are writing instructions for each other to negotiate the maze without bumping into any chairs. They have worked with Logo before, but they have always controlled the floor turtle in direct drive, without the use of procedures. Now they are being forced to plan a sequence of commands.

Idris and Pindhi are teaching their computer to play a tune. They have recently learned about procedures, and their unfinished version of 'Twinkle, Twinkle Little Star' is in the form of one very long procedure. The teacher is sitting with Idris and Pindhi, and she is hinting at the notion of sub-procedures. She is hoping that the boys might write separate procedures for the different lines of the tune and then put them together at the end.

Rebecca and Alison are driving a crane made from Lego. They have a control board attached to their computer, and the crane is wired to the board. They are using Logo together

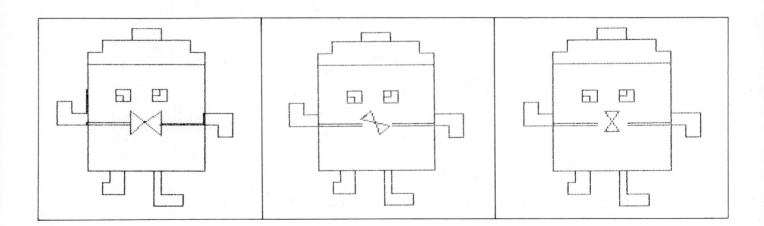

FIGURE 1.2   A screendump of Dusty Bin

with a control microworld. This extra software provides new commands which allow the girls to turn various motors on and off. The effect is to move the bucket forwards and backwards along the jib of the crane, to rotate the jib and to raise and lower the bucket. They are in the middle of writing a routine to instruct the crane to shift a pile of bricks from one end of the table to the other.

'What a magnificent crane!'

'Yes, we made it from Lego bricks last week.'

There is a group of four boys using a floor turtle with the third computer. Two of them are sitting at the keyboard, controlling the movement of the turtle. The other two are on the floor, with the turtle, and they are making sure that the flex does not become tangled. The boys need to draw one more line to complete their house (Fig. 1.3).

'Try FD 100.'

'That's not enough.'

'It doesn't matter — we can always do some more afterwards.'

The children do not know the length of the line that they need, and so their strategy is to make the turtle draw lines which are too short rather than too long. They are homing in on the correct length.

In fact the children had started this project by drawing a castle, and the sketch of their plans is to be seen in their exercise books. But, when they typed the commands at the keyboard, there was a bug. They were about to seek it out, when one of the boys suggested that the actual drawing looked quite like a house. Perhaps they should draw a house instead.

Mike chats to each of the groups of children in turn. The work that they are doing is very interesting, but what impresses him more than anything else is how articulate the children are. They all talk about their projects with ease, and they describe their failures as well as their successes in detail.

In the next classroom he visits, Mike is taken aback slightly. He had begun to accept it as normal practice that all the children worked on their own projects. But, in this classroom, the three pairs of children who are using Logo are all tackling the same challenge. The teacher has duplicated a sheet with one simple design on it (Fig. 1.4), and she has asked the children to find what they think is the best way to draw it on the screen. One of the pairs has started with the turtle at the bottom left-hand corner. They have not planned their work and they are writing a linear sequence of commands: FD 50 RT 90 FD 25 LT 90 FD 25 RT 90 FD 50... .

FIGURE 1.3   A floor turtle and child's picture

The children at another computer are having a long debate about the order in which the pattern should be traced. They have finally agreed that the design should be made from one big square, one small square and two perpendicular lines intersecting at the centre. One of the children wants to start with the outside square, but the other child is arguing that this will make it difficult to draw the cross. She wants to start at the centre.

The third pair of children is more experienced with Logo than the others, and they have decided to divide the picture into four identical quarters, each consisting of two squares. Once they have written a sub-procedure for a quarter, they will draw the complete design by repeating it four times.

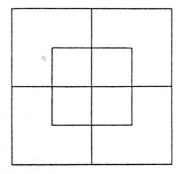

FIGURE 1.4   Design which children were asked to reproduce with Logo

The bell goes for morning break and Mike wanders down to the staff room with the teacher.

'Do you always give all the children the same task to do?' asks Mike, furtively hoping that he might be able to catch someone out at Bridgeton.

'Oh no. They spend most of their time working at their own projects. But it's useful to have a class discussion sometimes. When they've all had a go at the same design, I'll get them to look at each other's programs, and we'll talk about the different methods the children have adopted.'

'Is that why you have the computers close together?'

'Yes, that's right. They're normally scattered around the room, because I want the computer work to be integrated as much as possible. But for this exercise, I'm hoping that the pairs of children will learn from one another.'

'At the end will you tell the children the best way to do the drawing?'

'I'm not sure that there is one single, best way. One of the things I like so much about Logo is that there is never a wrong way to do something, and there are always lots of right ways.'

'But surely it's better to use sub-procedures than to have a long linear program?'

'Yes, but . . .'

The teacher is just about to answer Mike, when the bell rings to indicate the start of the next lesson. She interrupts herself to gulp down her coffee and to point Mike in the direction of some classes of older children, many of whom will be leaving school in 18 months' time.

Mike begins by sitting with two boys called Richard and Michael. They interrupt the execution of their program to talk to him.

'Hello, where are you from?'

'Oh, I teach at Fordham School.'

'Do you like it there?'

'. . . Well, yes . . . I do really.'

'I know some boys who go there — the teachers shout at you all the time.'

Mike thinks that this conversation has probably gone far enough, and so he changes the subject.

'What are those strange shapes darting about on your screen?'

'They're called sprites.'

'Why do they move when there's no program running?'

'Sprites are turtles which have speed. If you want them to stop, you can type SETSPEED Ø whenever you like.'

'How many different shapes can you have?'

'As many as you like. You can change the shape of any of the sprites yourself.'

'What do you do with sprites?'

'We're just messing about really. We've been getting them to move out from the centre of the screen, in different directions. It looks a bit like an explosion. Now we're trying to get the sprites to move back the other way. It's quite difficult because our first program was recursive, and we're not sure how to make it stop.'

'Do you think that a ball thrown across the park would move like a sprite?'

'I don't know really . . . . Those two girls over there are using their sprites to do things like that.'

Hayley and Donna are working towards a more clearly defined goal than Richard and Michael were. They have made a sprite into the shape of a circle, so that they can simulate the movement of a bouncing ball. They are using a newtonian microworld, which gives them some pre-programmed procedures to work with. They have used one of these procedures, SETFORCE, to make sure that the sprite will be influenced by gravity. Their present problem is rather similar to that of Richard and Michael. The girls have to decide how to stop the ball at the right time and then to make· it move in the opposite direction, but still under the influence of gravity.

Wendy and Darren are also using a microworld which provides them with extra procedures. It is called 3D, and it enables the children to imagine that they are moving their turtle in space. The drawings on the screen are in perspective. Wendy and Darren have just started working with 3D, and they do not yet fully understand the significance of the different sorts of turn (PITCH and ROLL) which the turtle can perform in three dimensions. They are trying to draw a cube, and their teacher has brought them some straws and pipe-cleaners so that they can make a skeletal model.

'We don't need to do this.'

'I think it might help if you do.'

'But we know what a cube looks like.'

'When you first used an ordinary turtle, you knew what a square looked like. But when you wanted the turtle to draw it, it was still helpful to walk around a big square.'

'But we can't walk round this little model.'

'No, but you can pretend that this rubber is the turtle, and let the turtle do the walking. It will help you decide what sort of turns you need.'

Later on Mike visits a class of 12- and 13-year olds who have all been using Logo for a few years. Their teacher is encouraging them to use Logo as another resource for the mathematics they are doing. There are three computers, and again they are scattered around the classroom. They have the same importance and the same status as any of the other pieces of mathematical equipment which are in use.

One of the other activities in the room is a game involving percentages. Kim and Rupa are just about to finish, and the teacher is talking to them about their work.

'How did you get on?'

'It was OK.'

'How did you work out three per cent of £14?'

'One per cent is 14p and we multiplied that by three.'

'And how did you do seven per cent of £50?'

'£100 would be 7p so it must be half of that.'

'Good. Next lesson I want you to try to write a Logo program that works out percentages for you. You'll find that you have to choose one method which will always work. That's called an algorithm.'

Kim and Rupa do not really understand the significance of the teacher's words yet, but they have enjoyed their game, and they are quite taken by the challenge of writing a Logo procedure to do the work for them.

Daniel is a very quiet boy and he is working on his own at one of the computers. He is using Logo to generate sequences of numbers. He has written a procedure which has two inputs, and he is studying the effect of changing their values. When Mike talks to him, Daniel explains how it all started as a calculator activity.

'We had to start with 80, find its square root, multiply by 2, and then do the same thing starting with the answer.'

'And then what?'

'Every time we got another answer, we wrote it down and repeated the process.'

'What happened?'

'The answers got closer and closer to 4.'

'Then what did you do?'

'Our investigation was to find out what happened when we started with other numbers.'

'Well?'

'It didn't seem to matter. The answers always got closer and closer to 4.'

'So why do you need the computer?'

'I want to find out what difference it makes when you multiply by 3 or 4 or some other number. My program lets me multiply by any number I want, and then it prints out all the answers.'

'And what have you found out?'

'I'm not sure yet. When you multiply by 3, the answers seem to get closer and closer to 9 ... .'

At another computer, Afzal and Suman are trying to draw a regular polygon with seven sides. They have drawn a hexagon, which has six sides, by typing REPEAT 6 [FD 50 RT 60]. A regular octagon was also quite easy. The angle was 45° and it had to be repeated eight times. But the boys are having some difficulty in finding the correct angle for the heptagon (Fig. 1.5). It seems to be around 50°, but they are very particular, and it is important that the lines join up precisely.

FIGURE 1.5 Difficulty experienced in drawing a regular heptagon

The boys are using trial-and-error methods to find the correct angles, but in a heptagon the angle is 360°/7 and so the result is not coming easily. As Mike stands behind the boys, he considers talking to them. If only they knew that the sum of the turns had to be 360°, the problem would be easy. But Mike is not sure what action to take. Should he simply tell them? Perhaps he should suggest a way for them to discover it for themselves. At Fordham School these sorts of questions do not seem to arise, and Mike just gets on with the job of teaching. But at Bridgeton it is all very different.

The third machine in this classroom is being used by two girls, Alison and Katrina, to continue an investigation. The children had been using sheets of circles with various numbers of points equally spaced around the circumference. They had been exploring the patterns obtained by jumping a set number of points. For instance, on a circle with ten points, jumping on four produces a star with five lines (Fig. 1.6). After the children had worked with the circle sheets for some time, the teacher had given them a simple procedure which was not difficult for Alison and Katrina to understand:

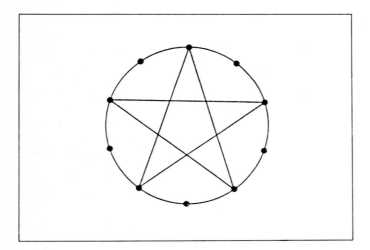

FIGURE 1.6   A star pattern


```
TO STAR "SIZE "ANGLE
   REPEAT 200 [FD :SIZE RT :ANGLE]
END
```

The teacher discusses it with the girls.
   'Can you see what the turtle will draw?'
   'It depends on SIZE and ANGLE.'
   'Yes it does. Why don't you run the procedure a few times. If you change the values of the two inputs, you'll begin to get the idea.'
The teacher wanders off and returns ten minutes later.
   'Do you see how it works now?'
   'Yes, it draws stars and some other shapes. Just like the investigation we were doing. The only trouble is that it keeps drawing over itself.'
   'What can you do about that?'
   'We've already tried making the number of REPEATs smaller. But sometimes you need more. It depends on ANGLE.'
   'Yes, the number of REPEATs has to be a function of ANGLE. If you can work out what the function is, you'll be able to get the turtle to stop as soon as it has finished each pattern.'
It is lunch-time, and Mike goes to the local pub with some of the teachers. They do not really want to spend their whole lunch-hour discussing school, but Mike does get the opportunity to hear some of the mathematics teachers' points of view.
   'Logo is wonderful for mathematics. The children are so well motivated.'
   'What mathematics do they learn through Logo?'
   'There's no set syllabus. It just depends what comes up.'
   'Didn't you plan any of the work that I saw?'
   'Not really. Those were the things the children chose to follow up. There are lots of topics in mathematics which they don't pursue with Logo. It's up to them. Some children don't use Logo at all in my lessons.'
   'But they aren't allowed to do their own projects, are they?'
   'No. They did that last year. They produced some amazing programs, but it did take a lot of time. I'm really not sure whether I'm doing the right thing though. Sometimes I think that some of the children did more mathematical thinking last year than they do now.'
   'I'm not sure I follow you.'
   'I've got another class where the children are 11 and 12. They do their own projects. At the moment one boy, Daniel, is designing a maze. He's done all the drawing, and he's set the turtle to move at the touch of a key. His final problem is to get the computer to respond if the user manages to get the turtle home. He has to work out a test to see whether the turtle is within a particular square on the screen. Now that is involving Daniel in all sorts of logical thinking, which would never have happened if I had insisted that his starting point had to be mathematical.'
   'What's going on at the other computer?'
   'Linda and Carol are drawing hedgehogs.'
   'That doesn't sound mathematical.'
   'It wasn't to start with. But now they've chosen to draw a family of hedgehogs. They are using a variable input to make the hedgehogs different sizes.'
   'What other mathematics do they do?'
   'Oh it's impossible to list it all. Anyway it's not just the content. They are thinking mathematically all the time when they do Logo.'
When the lunch-hour is over, the teachers walk back to their school and Mike leaves them to drive back to Fordham. He was going to stay all day, but he feels quite exhausted already. He has been bombarded with new ideas, and many of them seem quite radical. Mike agrees with the philosophy at Bridgeton School, and he is very excited about the Logo work going on there. But it is all so new for him, and he is not sure about the practicalities of introducing it at his own school. He needs time to assimilate everything, and he needs to talk to other sympathetic teachers who are in a similar position. Perhaps one or two people from his own school could make a similar visit to Bridgeton, and then they could get together afterwards.
   On the drive home, various negative thoughts flash through Mike's mind. How do they cope with examinations at Bridgeton School? How do they decide where to put the machines? What about security? How would they manage at Fordham? How could Logo possibly survive with that teacher who has complete silence in all his lessons? . . . Mike decides to put all this aside. He cannot possibly cope with it now. In any case it is no use thinking about the problems before deciding whether to introduce Logo into the curriculum. First of all, Mike must decide whether the positive aspects of Logo make any changes worthwhile.
   'Perhaps I'll give it a whirl in my own classroom', he muses.

A staff meeting

It is some months ago now that Mike visited Bridgeton. What he saw on that visit has had a lasting effect on him, even though he is now engrossed in his own problems at Fordham. He has been using Logo regularly, and several of the children that he teaches are now working on their own projects. He has also been thinking more about his own teaching style, and experimenting with allowing children to have more control over what happens in all his lessons.

Other teachers at Fordham have shown an interest in the Logo work that Mike's classes are doing. None of the other teachers has started using Logo yet, but some of them have visited Bridgeton, and one or two have been on courses about Logo. They are keen to try Logo, but they can foresee many problems. In order to air some of these worries, Mike is having a staff meeting about introducing Logo. Most of the staff of Fordham have come, including some of the senior staff; Sally, who has responsibility for computing, Bill, who has been at the school for many years and has a reputation for his strict discipline, and Sarah, an experienced teacher who is ready to listen to new ideas but is a little nervous about technology. Mike is also pleased to see Ursula, a probationer, and Trish, another young teacher who is very keen on Logo, sitting at the back. He has invited Josie, one of the teachers from Bridgeton, to join the meeting, to give him some moral support and practical advice.

Mike starts the meeting by expressing some general worries. As he finishes he catches Josie's eye and asks her to respond. Josie makes every effort to be reassuring.

'I can understand how some of you are feeling. We had lots of worries before we started Logo at Bridgeton, and we didn't get everything right first time, by any means. I'm afraid I don't have any easy solutions to offer. I can tell you how we resolved some of the problems, but what worked for us might not be any use to you. We certainly found that talking about things seemed to help.'

Everyone is still a little nervous, so Mike raises something specific that has been bothering him.

'I can't decide how to organise time for using the computer. I want to give the children long enough to do something useful, but I don't want them to have to wait too long between turns.'

'Why don't you organise a rota?', Ursula asks.

'I did think of that,' Mike replies, 'but a rota seems to be at odds with the classroom atmosphere that I saw at Bridgeton. It all seemed much more relaxed there.'

After a short silence, Josie comments,

'We tried several ways to make sharing the computers work, and to stop certain children monopolising the machines. No one thing seemed to work for everyone, because every classroom situation is different. In general, we found that younger children needed shorter, more frequent, spells at the machine. When I started, I gave a fairly short time for each group, and then I adjusted this to suit particular groups. I hate to have to stop groups in the middle of, say, de-bugging a procedure just because time is up.'

Sarah has a useful suggestion.

'I think I'd let my group make the arrangements for time sharing themselves. They're less likely to complain about its being unfair if they've made the decisions.'

But Bill is horrified.

'My little ones couldn't cope with that! I think I need to make decisions like that in my classroom.'

They go on discussing this together, but Trish asks Josie a direct question.

'What size groups do you find work best? I've seen children working in pairs at Bridgeton, but that means they have to wait longer for their next turn.'

'Well, if the children work in bigger groups, they can have more time at the computer, but how well a large group can cooperate depends on personalities and, of course, the experience the children have of working together. We found that, when children are working with a floor turtle, groups of four seem to be all right. But, for a screen turtle, pairs really are best; even three at the keyboard is too many. I prefer to allow children to form their own working groups, and to change them when they want to, but of course there can be difficulties with dominant personalities and differences in ability. There are some children who want to work on their own at times, so it's nice to be able to allow some flexibility.'

The teachers who have the youngest children in the school have a different problem.

'We haven't got as many computers yet as Bridgeton has; not even enough for one in each classroom. We're going to have to share machines.'

This is something that Mike has already given some thought to.

'It's going to be hard to give everyone a 'fair' share. I think there is a danger of spreading the computer time too thinly, so that none of the children really get much from it. I'm quite sure, from the bit I've done already, that the children need quite a lot of time with Logo, and they do learn from being able to watch each other working. You may not agree with this, but I think it would be best to concentrate the machines in some classes to begin with, and then perhaps to move them to other classes for the next term.'

'That seems a bit hard!', complains Bill, 'Some of the children won't get to use the computers for ages. I think some of the parents might be a bit cross. After all, they did all help with the fund raising.'

Other teachers can see Mike's point, but Sarah expresses another problem.

'If we do put several machines in one room, some of us will have to use machines that run different versions of Logo. Isn't that going to cause enormous problems? I mean, I don't think any of mine can even type.'

Mike has already had to cope with this. He explains that he has been using two different machines in his classroom this term.

'In practice, it hasn't been much of a problem so far. The children seem to cope with the different versions of Logo more easily than I do. They just see them as part of the machine, like the different keyboard layouts.'

Sally, who is in charge of computing, joins in this discussion with mixed feelings.

'I know the children soon get used to different keyboards. After all, they use a variety of different machines already, but aren't there more serious differences in different versions of Logo, Josie?'

Josie explains that this is something they have had to cope with at Bridgeton as well.

'We don't really find it a problem now. The children are able to transfer relatively easily from one version to another, but they do need to understand that you can't transfer files on disc between two different machines. So children need to stick to one machine while they're working on a particular project.

'Most of the differences in the implementation of Logo are very small. For example, the command to move the turtle backwards is BD in some versions, and BK in others, or to send the turtle to the centre of the screen it may be CT or HOME. There are other differences that are more significant: there is a difference in the way REPEAT is used in some versions, for instance. It doesn't make much difference in the early stages, though it could be important for some of your more advanced pupils, Sally. We can talk about it in more detail sometime, if you want to.

'I would like to say one more thing about sharing machines, if that's all right Mike. I think it's very important that whatever arrangements you make, they must be open to change. However carefully you plan, you're not likely to get a system that works smoothly first time. We certainly didn't! And we found that even arrangements that worked well when Logo was first introduced didn't always work so well as the children became more experienced and more involved in their own projects.'

Sally, and some of the other teachers at the top of the school, have a different problem about access to machines. The machines that they can use are all in the computer room, where there is a network of ten machines, linked to a file server (that acts like a disc drive) and a printer. At the moment, classes are timetabled to use the room for computer studies, and a few other lessons, and children are sometimes allowed to use the machines in break times. There has already been some fairly heated discussion about whether or not the network should be split up, and the machines distributed among several classrooms, so Mike is a bit apprehensive about saying anything. He is relieved when Josie has some comments to make.

'We did have a network at Bridgeton when we first started working with Logo, and some of our staff liked it a lot. It does have some advantages. All the children can do Logo at the same time, so you don't have to worry about a rota, or about having to organise different kinds of activities for other groups. Because they all share a disc drive, it's also easy for children to load each other's files and to look at them, so you can encourage them to learn from each other. But after a while we felt that the network made it more difficult to integrate Logo with other work, and it gave the computer an artificial importance. We decided to break up our network, and put a few machines in each room, and now I think we all prefer it.'

It looks as though the argument might start again, but Ursula changes the subject slightly.

'I think I'd prefer to use the network so that I know Sally will take care of the machines. I'm not too keen on having computers in my own room because I'm not sure I can cope with setting them up. And I'd be really worried in case something went wrong.'

Sally is used to reassuring colleagues about worries like this.

'It wouldn't be sensible to go into details now about how to set up different machines. Let's find a time when I can go through it all with you. It really isn't difficult. You'll need to know how to get Logo started, and how to save your work on disc. If you've got a printer in your room, I can show you how to use it to print out drawings and programs. You may also want to use a floor turtle, which has to be linked to the computer, and there are a few special commands which relate to the turtle. The main thing to remember is that you are unlikely to do any damage while you are learning to use the machines. You can't do any harm to the machine by typing something wrong. It is possible to delete a file from the disc, but you are unlikely to do this by accident. I'll show you how to delete files, to put your mind at rest. The only real safety measure you need to remember is never to turn the power on or off with a disc still in the disc drive, as that can damage the information stored on the disc. There are plenty of handbooks around, which have all the information in, but it will be easier and quicker if I help you at first. Actually, there are probably a few people who would like to go through it all from the beginning. I'm sure you'll find you can help each other while you are getting familiar with everything.'

There are several grateful comments from around the room, and Mike offers to give any help he can, although he is not completely confident about handling machines yet. He too has worries about machines breaking down.

'Could you say a bit about the network, Sally? And about machines going wrong: that still worries me, and I can't just call for you in the middle of a lesson.'

'Well, the network isn't much different really. I can show you how to load Logo, and how to use the printer, and you should be able to run a floor turtle from a machine on the network: I'll sort that out.

'As for breaking down, it can be very frustrating for you and for the children. I've had to go in a corner to let off steam a few times, but it's really much less likely than you imagine, unless the machines are badly misused. Have you had many problems with your machines, Josie?'

'We had a few at first, when we were getting used to them, but nothing serious. Most problems can be put right fairly simply, I think. We do find that a few basic routines help to minimise accidental problems. For example, we always encourage the children to handle machines carefully, and not to lean on keyboards or to hit keys randomly if things seem to be going wrong. As a last resort, most problems can be cured by turning the machine off (don't forget to take the disc out!) and starting again, but that does mean that you lose everything in the machine's memory. Now I encourage children to save their work at regular intervals so that, if we do have to turn off, they don't lose too much.'

Josie and Sally both sound confident and reassuring, but lots of people still have worries that they want to discuss.

Despite all her teaching experience, Sarah is feeling anxious about her lack of knowledge of Logo.

'Some of the children in my group already have computers at home, and they know a lot more about them than I do. I know Mike knew quite a bit about Logo before he started using it with children, but I'm really only going to be one step ahead, and I'm sure the children will soon overtake me. If they start asking me questions I can't answer, I'll be in a real panic! I did try looking at the handbook, but it seems to be written for computer experts.'

Several others mutter in agreement: Bill's voice comes through.

'I don't think I can teach anything properly if I don't understand it myself.'

Mike feels a bit unsure about how to answer this.

'It's true that I have done a bit of Logo myself before I introduced it to the children, but it is getting to the stage now when some of them want to do things I haven't done. I feel a bit anxious about that at times . . . . We have worked on some things together, and I've learnt as much as the children have, but I'm sure that means I'm missing a lot of opportunities to suggest ways they could develop their own projects.'

Josie is quick to come in here.

'I don't think you should worry too much about that, Mike. One of the nice things about Logo is that you can learn alongside the children. Of course you may miss opportunities, but I think that's true of anything you teach for the first time. You're bound to get better at seeing the possibilities as you have more experience with Logo. Several of my colleagues knew very little Logo when they started, but I think the children gained quite a lot from seeing their teacher working with new ideas. It does help to break down the barriers a bit, and make the children more willing to admit when they get stuck.'

The atmosphere is more relaxed now, and comments come thick and fast. Many of these are not to do with practicalities, but reflect different sorts of worries.

'I think I can see the point of letting the children choose their own projects to work on, but what if they just mess about, and don't settle down to anything? I can only give them a short time each week at the machine, and I'm worried that some of them will just waste it. I don't want to force them to do something they don't want to, but ...'

'If the children are all working on their own projects, I can't see how I'll be able to make sure that they all cover the same work. Would it be better to go through each new command with the whole class, so that I know that they've all done it?'

'We have to cover a set syllabus each term, and I'm afraid that we won't get through it if the children spend too much time on their Logo projects. Someone is bound to complain if I leave something out!'

'It's easy to see which commands the children need to know at the beginning, but I'm not sure which ones come next, and which order they should learn them in.'

'If I always let the children work in groups, some of mine will just sit back and let the others do all the work. I'll need to give some kind of test, or I won't be sure that they've learnt anything.'

'The children have to learn so much at the beginning that they'll need my attention all the time. But what about the rest of the class? They'll be all over the place!'

'When I visited a Logo lesson at Bridgeton, it seemed very haphazard. Some of the children were doing wonderful things, but others were just fiddling about. There didn't seem to be any structure to the lesson, and I couldn't see what some of it was leading to. The teacher said that she didn't think it was right to intervene too much, but I think some of the children were making a lot of mistakes and not really getting anywhere.'

'My class are so easily disturbed by anything out of the ordinary, that I think that just having two computers will be very disruptive. If only a few children are using them, I'm sure the others won't concentrate properly on their own work. They'll be out of their seats half the time, trying to see what's going on.'

'I want the children to think out how to do things, like drawing a circle for themselves, without me telling them what to do. But if they can get each other's work from the disc, they might just copy.'

'My class don't know much about angles yet, or how to use protractors. I'll have to do a lot of work on degrees before they use the turtle, or they won't understand how to turn it.'

'I've seen what other schools have done with Logo, and it all looks wonderful, but I'm sure my children couldn't cope with work like that. Most of them can hardly spell 'forward', and none of them knows how to type. I'm afraid they may get frustrated with silly mistakes.'

As Josie had suggested at the start of the meeting, talking about these worries did seem to make people feel better, even though no one could suggest solutions straight away.

Making changes

The discussion we have described in this imaginary staff meeting is based on many such conversations we have had with teachers when they begin using Logo. We have put them together here not in order to offer answers to all the questions they raise (although some of them may be discussed further in later chapters), but simply to say that these uncertainties are shared by many teachers.

All the comments towards the end of the meeting have something in common: they reflect the fact that working with Logo may mean making changes in the way that you work in the classroom. How big these changes are will depend on the way that you normally work and the kind of school you are in. But being faced with such changes, big or small, makes us all feel insecure. It can happen with lots of things in school; changing to a new scheme or textbook, teaching a different age group, joining a new school, breaking in a new headteacher. Probably the most helpful single thing you can do is to share that insecurity with other teachers in the same position. We cannot help you to do that through the pages of a book, so do try to find someone to talk to, in your own school or through groups or courses in your LEA.

It may be useful to focus on what it is about working with Logo that forces us to make changes in our teaching style. The key seems to be that the children take over control of the learning situation. Handing over control goes against many of our existing ideas about what being a teacher means, and it can be disturbing. It takes time to get used to, for the children as well as the teacher. Many of their existing ideas about how teachers behave may be undermined, particularly if they are not used to being given any choice about what they do in the classroom.

Working with Logo does involve making changes, and this may not be easy. If you like the idea of children in your school using Logo, we hope that you will want to face this challenge, and that the rest of this book will give you some help.

2 Children's Work

In this chapter we want to describe the sort of things that children do when they are programming with Logo. There will be some commentary too, but the main emphasis of the chapter will be to describe the projects and other work which the children in our own classes have done. Since we are only using real examples, from our own experience, we ought to start by giving a little background information.

Trinity School in Leamington Spa, Warwickshire, was described briefly in the Introduction. It is a secondary school, and much of our work has been with 11- and 12-year-old children. One of us taught Logo to a first-year class for two 70 minute sessions each week, and the following year the other taught a similar group for one session a week. Both of these groups were using a network, with several machines in the same room, and so the children had plenty of time to explore and to develop projects. We have also taught some older children, and there are a few examples in this chapter from 14- and 15-year-olds. Our work has been almost entirely dependent on the screen turtle. We have mostly used RML Logo[1] and Logotron Logo[2], without any additional hardware or software.

Drawing pictures

When we organised our early session of playing turtle, and using the single floor turtle with the whole class, we were careful to avoid too much emphasis on mathematical shapes. We drew pictures so that the children would start their independent work at the computer in the same way. We wanted them to learn to form their own goals and to develop projects right from the start. Also, in the early stages we felt that it was important that the children were working in an environment which allowed them to explore lengths and angles without being constrained by the geometry of particular shapes. We thought that it was important that they became comfortable with the turtle and the dimensions of the screen that they were using, so that they knew whether to type FD 20 or FD 200, and so that they could distinguish between RT 10 and RT 100. We did not want to plunge into abstract ideas at the expense of the children's control.

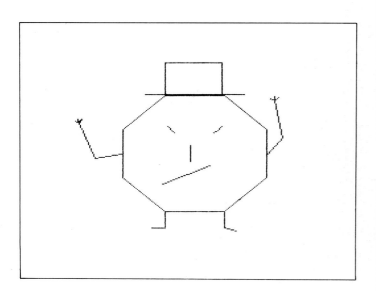

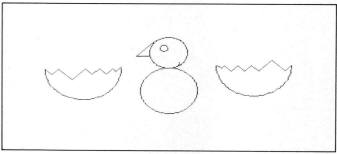

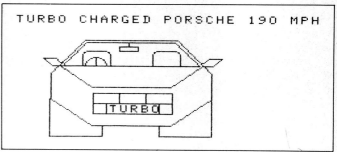

FIGURE 2.1 Examples of drawings produced by children with Logo

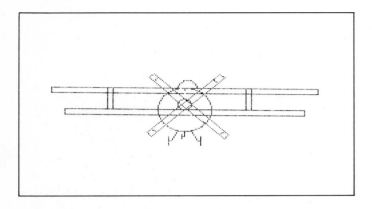

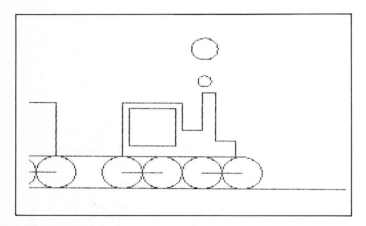
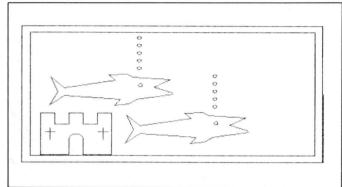

FIGURE 2.1 (cont)   Examples of drawings produced by children with Logo

We certainly did not forbid the children to draw patterns, but we did not tell them about the possibility either, and so in the very early stages the children's screens were full of cars and boats and houses and flowers (Fig. 2.1). Most of the programs for these pictures were written in a linear style. For instance, Katrina and Alison's boat (Fig. 2.2) was called MARY.ROSE, and they used many sub-procedures: OUTLINE, FUN-NELL, CABIN, OUTSIDE, ANCHOR, SMOKE and WAVES.

The sub-procedures which the girls wrote did not exhibit any structure, and for each one the starting position of the turtle was exactly where it finished in the previous sub-procedure. The sub-procedures could not really be tested independently, since they had to be used in the order in which they were written. In fact, the girls probably only used sub-procedures because the whole thing would otherwise have been too long to fit in the computer's memory. None of this is surprising, because there is very little in the picture which could benefit from more structure. The windows might have warranted a sub-procedure to themselves, but there are only three of them, and the girls may not have decided to draw the third window before the first two were finished. All this is true for most of the children's early pictures — there was very little structure in the programs because structure was unnecessary.

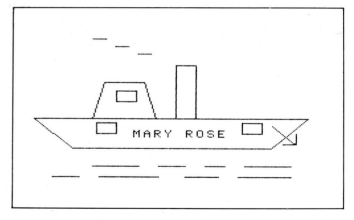

```
TO MARY.ROSE
   OUTLINE
   FUNNELL
   CABIN
   OUTSIDE
   ANCHOR
   SMOKE
   WAVES
END
```

FIGURE 2.2   The use of sub-procedures to draw a ship

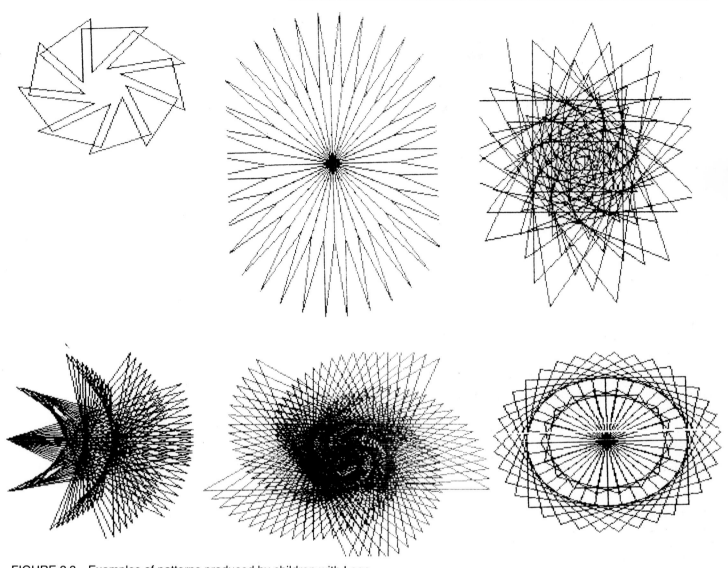

FIGURE 2.3   Examples of patterns produced by children with Logo

Random patterns

Some children continued to draw pictures for a long time, and they were able to get their turtles to produce wonderful detail, but others were seduced much earlier by Logo's patterns, which are very quick and easy to create (examples are shown in Fig. 2.3).

With the LCSI version of Logo there is a wrap-around facility on the screen and, in the very early stages, many children took great delight in turning the turtle slightly from its initial heading and then typing FD 100000. In an instant, the screen was full of diagonal lines (Fig. 2.4). The effect was easily achieved, and the powerful feeling was prolonged by changing the colour of the screen turtle's pen, turning the turtle a fraction once again, and repeating the process. A new set of

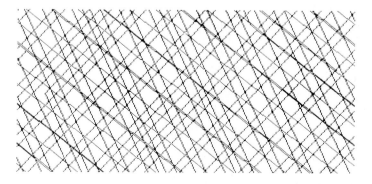

FIGURE 2.4   Example of a pattern produced by using screen wrap-around

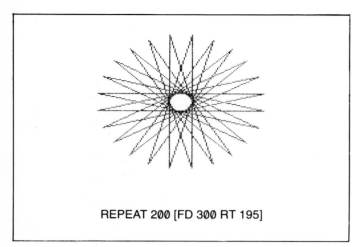

REPEAT 200 [FD 300 RT 195]

FIGURE 2.5   Example of a pattern produced using the REPEAT command

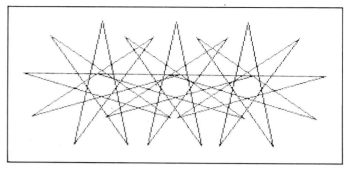

```
TO QAZ
  SETPC 1
  REPEAT 9 [FD 420 LT 160]
  BK 390
  SETPC 2
  REPEAT 9 [FD 420 LT 160]
  FD 192
  SETPC 3
  REPEAT 9 [FD 420 LT 160]
  HT
END
```

FIGURE 2.6   Example of a pattern produced using the REPEAT command

parallel lines then appeared at a different orientation. The children often persisted with this activity until the screen was full of colour.

This type of early activity should not be condemned, even though it may not appear to have very much educational value. Children will need a period of play with any new piece of equipment, and the computer is no different. In fact it is likely to be helpful for the children to play with all the new commands that they learn in the same way. Children need to explore what a new command does, and how it works. This is naturally achieved by testing it to its limits:

'What is the biggest number that I can use with the FD command? . . .'

'What is the most complicated star that I can draw with REPEAT? . . .'

Many children learned of the REPEAT command after only a few sessions at the computer, and they quickly realised its potential for making patterns easily by repeatedly drawing a line and turning through an angle (Figs. 2.5 and 2.6). Once the children had learned about procedures, they created further designs by defining a shape of some sort and then repeatedly calling it (Fig. 2.7).

Others used a different technique for the creation of similar random patterns. Children often learned about recursion by accident, typing the title line again as the last line of the procedure while still in the editor. Later, some children used recursion deliberately to devise patterns which were not planned in advance. The children typed in their procedure without any clear idea of the outcome and then altered it slightly, changing a length here and an angle there, until they were pleased enough with the result to get a screendump from the printer (some examples are shown in Fig. 2.8).

Initially, the problem with recursive procedures is that they cannot be used for any further construction. This is because they continue indefinitely, and the only way to stop them is to press the escape key, or whichever button the computer uses to interrupt a program and to return control to the user. At a higher level, some children learned to control recursive procedures with the IF command, but at this early stage the only option open when the children considered a pattern to be finished was to start something new. If, however, a procedure is constructed with REPEAT, it can then be used to develop a more complex design later. In the work shown in Fig. 2.9, Arifa and Clare have used REPEAT in the procedure called FISH, and FISH has been used within CRAFT. CRAFT filled the screen, and so it did not really matter that it was recursive and had no further application.

Some children who continued to use REPEAT were able to build up programs with many layers of sub-procedures, each new procedure being repeated to form another. These programs, which were not planned at all, exhibited a high degree of structure. The style of programming was bottom up, since the children built the sub-procedures and modified them before using them within the super-procedures (Fig. 2.10).

Getting the right balance

These two sorts of early activity, creating pictures and drawing patterns, are at opposite ends of a spectrum. The pictures were planned to some extent, whereas the patterns were not. When the children drew pictures, they may have added new ideas as they worked, or changed their existing plans, but there was always some overall direction that they had chosen for themselves. The patterns, however, developed according to whatever satisfied the children after they had drawn the patterns on the screen. The work to draw pictures was goal

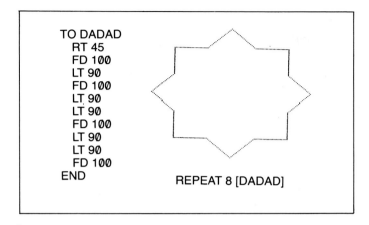

```
TO DADAD
  RT 45
  FD 100
  LT 90
  FD 100
  LT 90
  LT 90
  FD 100
  LT 90
  LT 90
  FD 100
END
```

REPEAT 8 [DADAD]

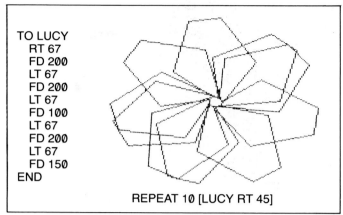

```
TO LUCY
  RT 67
  FD 200
  LT 67
  FD 200
  LT 67
  FD 100
  LT 67
  FD 200
  LT 67
  FD 150
END
```

REPEAT 10 [LUCY RT 45]

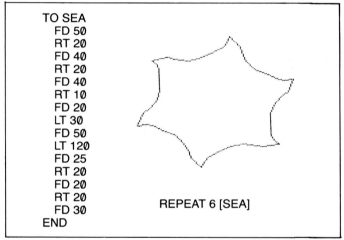

```
TO SEA
  FD 50
  RT 20
  FD 40
  RT 20
  FD 40
  RT 10
  FD 20
  LT 30
  FD 50
  LT 120
  FD 25
  RT 20
  FD 20
  RT 20
  FD 30
END
```

REPEAT 6 [SEA]

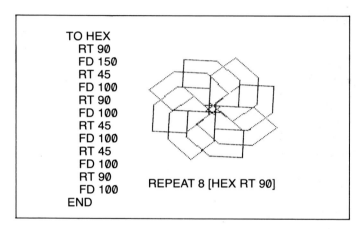

```
TO HEX
  RT 90
  FD 150
  RT 45
  FD 100
  RT 90
  FD 100
  RT 45
  FD 100
  RT 45
  FD 100
  RT 90
  FD 100
END
```

REPEAT 8 [HEX RT 90]

FIGURE 2.7   Examples of patterns produced when children REPEAT their own procedures

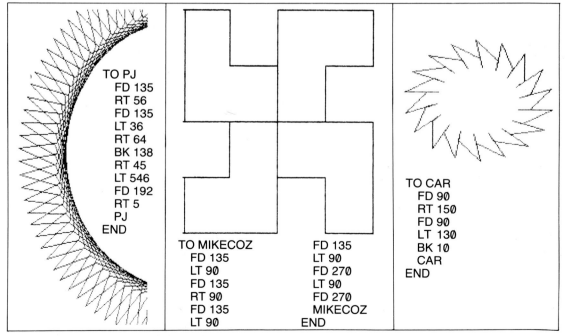

```
TO PJ
  FD 135
  RT 56
  FD 135
  LT 36
  RT 64
  BK 138
  RT 45
  LT 546
  FD 192
  RT 5
  PJ
END
```

```
TO MIKECOZ
  FD 135
  LT 90
  FD 135
  RT 90
  FD 135
  LT 90

  FD 135
  LT 90
  FD 270
  LT 90
  FD 270
  MIKECOZ
END
```

```
TO CAR
  FD 90
  RT 150
  FD 90
  LT 130
  BK 10
  CAR
END
```

FIGURE 2.8   Examples of patterns produced using recursion

```
TO CRAFT
   FISH
   LT 5
   CRAFT
END

TO FISH
   REPEAT 9 [FD 400 LT 160]
END
```

FIGURE 2.9   Example of a pattern produced with REPEAT and recursion

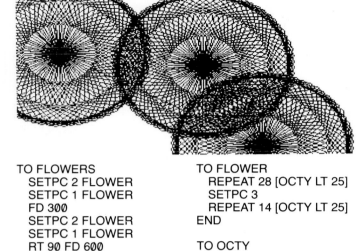

```
TO FLOWERS                    TO FLOWER
   SETPC 2 FLOWER                REPEAT 28 [OCTY LT 25]
   SETPC 1 FLOWER                SETPC 3
   FD 300                        REPEAT 14 [OCTY LT 25]
   SETPC 2 FLOWER             END
   SETPC 1 FLOWER
   RT 90 FD 600               TO OCTY
   SETPC 2 FLOWER                REPEAT 8 [FD 100 LT 45]
   SETPC 1 FLOWER             END
END
```

FIGURE 2.10   Example of a more complicated pattern produced using several sub-procedures

FIGURE 2.11   A row of houses drawn using recursion

directed, and making patterns was an exploratory activity. The two programming styles were also very different. Drawing patterns involved a bottom-up approach, and the final procedures were often clean and elegant. The programs for the early pictures were mostly linear.

The children needed to achieve some balance between these aspects, and we found that this happened far more readily when the starting point was a picture. Firstly, the children's motivation was rarely in jeopardy when they were drawing pictures. Children who were flitting from one unplanned pattern to another lost interest much more quickly. Also, the children found it difficult to plan an abstract design, whereas structured work often developed naturally from pictures. Some able children did manage to draw grids and tiling patterns, but most children needed a context in which they could develop a more-structured approach to their work as it became necessary. The following sections will illustrate how drawing pictures did lead to more advanced thinking skills.

Rows of houses

When a child has drawn one house, it is likely that she will want to use her procedure to draw a street. Unlike the windows in Katrina and Alison's boat, a house will be complicated enough for the child not to want to type the whole thing six or seven times. This forces the child to find some sort of structure for her program.

Daniel and Michael used recursion to design the row of houses shown in Fig. 2.11. There are four procedures called H, H2, H3 and H4. H draws the walls and the roof, and its final command is H2. H2 draws another part of the house, and then calls H3. Similarly, H3 calls H4, and finally H4 completes the house before calling H again. The boys used REPEAT to draw each window and the walls. Their teacher suggested that they might draw two rows of houses, one on either side of the street. This was an attempt to get them to control the program by repeating H, rather than using recursion, but the children did not take up the idea.

Suman was working at what appeared to be the same level as the other children in his under-achieving fourth-year class when he suddenly took off. He became totally immersed in his drawing of a street, and he worked at it continuously for over two weeks. This was in stark contrast to the others in that group, who had never shown any concern for their previous work. Suman announced the completion of his work by labelling it 'PLAY SCHOOL' (Fig. 2.12) and he used the humour of this comment as an excuse to show off his work to anyone who would pay attention.

Suman's work actually started with a castle. He had done a quick sketch in his book, but his procedure had a bug somewhere, and the result looked more like a house (Fig. 2.13). Suman was not too attached to the castle at this stage, and so he changed the title of his procedure to HOUSE and

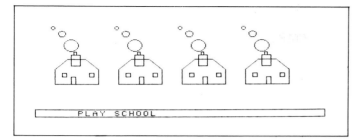

FIGURE 2.12   A row of houses that started as a castle (Fig. 2.13)

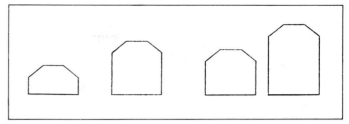

FIGURE 2.14   Houses of different heights (a stage intermediate between those of Figs. 2.12 and 2.13)

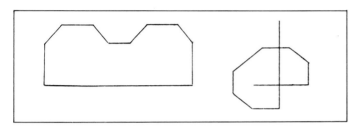

FIGURE 2.13   The castle, produced by a procedure with a bug in it, that eventually became the houses in Fig. 2.12

made the small amendments which were necessary. Children often change their goals when they are working with Logo. When a job is difficult, it is natural to modify the task as well as the way it is being tackled.

The next stage in Suman's project was to draw four houses of different heights. Although his house was not really finished, Suman had recently learned about the use of variables in procedures. He used one to determine the height of the house and another for its position on the screen (Fig. 2.14).

Suman continued by writing CHIMNEY, WINDOW, DOOR, ROAD and SMOKE. With the exception of ROAD, these all had two variable inputs, and their purpose was to enable Suman to place the various parts of the houses in the correct positions on the screen. Initially, Suman had one super-procedure called STREET, which became longer and longer as his project developed. In order to make his programming more manageable, Suman developed intermediate procedures. Thus HOUSES was written to call HOUSE four times, and STREET was amended to incorporate HOUSES as a sub-procedure.

This structure was necessary because STREET had become too long to edit easily. After each small change, Suman had to wait too long while the complete image was drawn on the screen. His intermediate procedures enabled him to test HOUSES independently. The final product of Suman's work — 13 procedures welded together in a highly structured way — is most impressive. Yet he was never taught to work so methodically. Neither the drawing nor the structure was planned in advance. The approach was bottom up, and Suman learned to apply more structure when he needed it.

Letters and numbers

As you can see from the names in Fig. 2.15, the activity of drawing letters and numbers was more popular with girls than with boys. Girls often enjoyed writing messages on the screen with the LABEL command, which is available in RML Logo, but the print is small, and to draw larger letters they had to use the turtle. This activity has great potential for structured work, but the girls who chose it tended to be less able, and the results here are not striking. In most cases the children used a different sub-procedure for each letter, but they were not written independently, so they could only be used within the one particular word which was being designed. Perhaps this is inevitable, since it was not possible to fit more than two or three words on the screen at any one time. It is a much more advanced enterprise to think in terms of a program which clears the screen and displays many different words.

Rachel and Andrew were students intending to become teachers, and their long project did involve this idea. They were designing a spelling test for young children, and they needed to be able to draw many different words. They wrote all their letter procedures so that the turtle started at the bottom left-hand corner of each letter and finished in the correct position for the subsequent letter to be drawn. This meant that the children would be able to type any sequence of letters to get the word of their choice drawn on the screen. After this, Rachel and Andrew wrote a single procedure to draw any given word, and then they added a test so that the word would be drawn on a new line if it was too long to fit on the screen.

Blocks of colour

Some versions of Logo have a FILL command, for filling an enclosed area with colour. All the child has to do is to move the turtle inside the area and then type FILL. Thankfully, this was not available on either of the versions which we were using. (Logotron have produced an extension disc which contains FILL, but the children did not know this.) As a result, many children learned a great deal, making blocks of colour by teaching the turtle to draw lots and lots of straight lines (Fig. 2.16).

FIGURE 2.15 Examples of letters and numbers produced using Logo

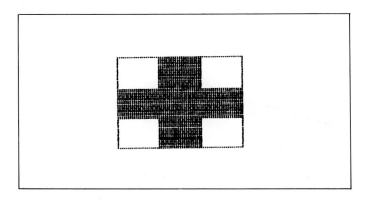

FIGURE 2.16   Blocks of colour produced by many straight lines

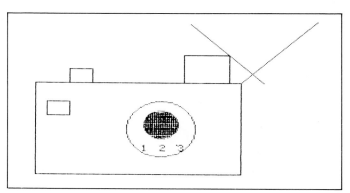

FIGURE 2.17   A camera with a filled circle produced using recursion

```
TO LINE "HEIGHT
  FD :HEIGHT
  BK :HEIGHT
  RT 90 FD 1 LT 90
END
```

His teacher challenged him to draw other filled shapes and, untypically, he became absorbed by this abstract mathematical problem. He was obviously in command of his work, because he succeeded in drawing a parallelogram very easily by adding one extra command to his LINE procedure. He inserted FD 2 at the beginning and changed the title of the other procedure from RECT to PARA.

A triangle proved to be more difficult, because all the lines have to be drawn with different lengths, but, despite the fact that Richard had not achieved wonderful results in the past, the following two procedures taken at the end of subsequent lessons show admirable attempts:

```
TO TRI "LEN "ANG
  IF :LEN > 1000 [STOP]
  FD :LEN LT :ANG
  BK :LEN RT :ANG
  RT 90 FD 1 LT 90
  TRI :LEN+1 :ANG
END

TO TRI "S "R
  CS HT
  FD :S LT 110
  FD :R LT 140
  FD :R LT 110
  IF :S=0 [TRI 80 80]
  TRI :S-1 :R-1
END
```

There were many more examples of this sort of work which we were not able to print. One boy, Steve, designed a complete picture from blocks of different colours. One green block provided the grass at the foot of the screen, and another blue block was used for the sky. He then used further colours for trees and houses. Unfortunately, without a colour printer, it is not possible to get a screendump other than as a large black rectangle!

In order to achieve these effects, the children usually realised that they had to write a procedure to draw one line, which they could then repeat. The main difficulty which the children faced was knowing exactly what to repeat. As they wrote the procedure for the single line, they did not always understand that the turtle needed to finish in the correct position, ready to draw the next line.

Two particular projects which utilised this technique are worth describing in more detail. Richard started in the usual way and with plenty of help to control the variables, he managed to draw rectangular blocks of various sizes:

```
TO RECT "WIDTH "HEIGHT
  REPEAT :WIDTH [LINE :HEIGHT]
END
```

Another example of the use of blocks of colour occurred when Annabel and Linda were drawing a camera (Fig. 2.17). The girls wanted to fill in the lens cap, and they achieved this by drawing a number of concentric circles of decreasing radius.

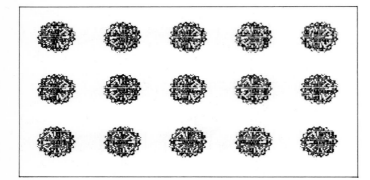

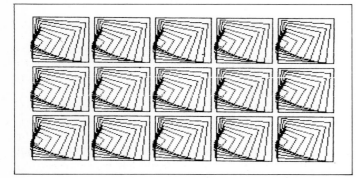

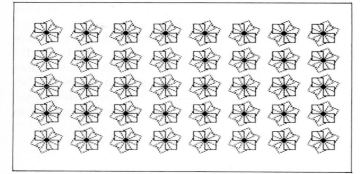

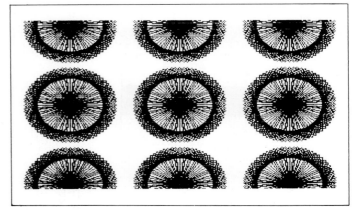

FIGURE 2.18   Examples of wallpaper patterns produced using Logo

```
TO S
  CS RT 90
  PU SETPOS [−600 320] PD
  REPEAT 6 [X]
END

TO X
  REPEAT 10 [Z]
  PU BK 900 RT 90 FD 90 LT 90 PD
END

TO Z
  REPEAT 9 [FD 60 LT 160]
  PU FD 90 PD
END
```

Although RML Logo provided the girls with procedures for drawing specified circles (ARCL and ARCR), their program was very advanced. They had to use recursion, and they had to control it properly so that they could use their procedure within the overall program.

Impressive though this work was, we have described it here to contrast it with Annabel's attitude in the subsequent lesson. Her partner was absent then, and Annabel was whiling away some time by drawing rectangular blocks of colour. She was with another child who was less able than she was and who had recently come across variables for the first time. When their teacher suggested that they vary the width of the blocks, Annabel said 'Oh Ronnie, you're just trying to make it difficult for us!'

By any normal, objective standards, the work that her teacher was asking Annabel and her temporary partner to do was much easier than everything she had demonstrated the lesson before. So why did she describe it as difficult? A significant factor must surely be that the task was unimportant to her. She did not have the slightest commitment to it, and she did not see any point in struggling. When children are engaged in their own projects, as Annabel was with Linda when they were drawing a camera, they are much more willing to persist with difficult ideas.

Wallpaper patterns

One activity which does stem from patterns rather than pictures is the creation of wallpaper designs. The last example in Fig. 2.18, by Daniel and Anthony, was certainly the most efficient. They wrote three procedures Z, X and S. The procedure Z draws the motif once and moves the turtle on ready to draw the next one. X produces a single row of stars by repeating Z ten times and then moving the turtle to the start of the next row. S, the main super-procedure, clears the screen, places the turtle at the correct starting position and calls X six times to draw the six rows.

If the children know from the start that they will want to repeat a design on the screen several times, they are bound to look for a structured approach, which is more efficient than a linear string of commands. However, this is not an easy task, and most children produced code which occupied several pages and which was far less structured than Daniel and Anthony's. In common with all the work being described in this chapter, the creation of wallpaper patterns would not have been suitable for all the children. Some were not interested and others, who were not able to apply more structure, would have found it tedious and frustrating. But there were occasions when more able children were playing with random patterns, and it was not inappropriate to offer a challenge of this sort. The atmosphere in the classroom was such that the children always knew that they did not have to accept.

Simulating movement

The machines we were using did not have a FILL command, and so the children had to create their own routines. Similarly, there were no sprites available to us, and so if the children wanted movement they had to simulate it for themselves. Many projects developed around the difficult task of repeatedly drawing a shape and rubbing it out in many different places. Of course, the movement which the children were able to generate for themselves was far less realistic than that which might have been achieved with sprites. Logo is still a fairly slow language for computers to operate. It takes far too long for anything complicated to be drawn and then rubbed out for the resulting effect to be realistic.

This may have discouraged some of the older children, but the 11- and 12-year-olds were not deterred. They were perfectly content to choose simple shapes, which could be drawn relatively quickly, and, if the final effect was still not quite true to life, it did not matter. The important thing was that they had done it themselves. Younger children get involved in their tasks readily, but even older children and students (and adults) can be quite happy to ignore any lack of realism if the task is engaging. When Rachel and Andrew were spending time in their university course designing a spelling test for small children, we knew that it was most unlikely that it would ever be used in a classroom. Rachel and Andrew probably knew that too, although of course we certainly did not say this to them explicitly. Somehow it just did not seem to matter.

The first big project in one of our classes which involved movement was Dusty Bin. Annabel and Leena worked consistently for ten weeks. (They had access to the computer for 2 hours and 20 minutes each week.) During this time they

drew the cartoon character on the screen and then made the bow-tie spin. Towards the end of their project they made the arms revolve and the legs walk up and down. The climax of their work was the spinning tie, and they had many struggles to achieve this. Annabel wrote about the project for our classroom display and her write-up is shown in Fig. 2.19.

The first major problem which Annabel and Leena encountered with their spinning tie was how to rub it out. They had written a procedure called BOW, which drew the tie once. They could have simply typed PE (pen erase) and written another different procedure to go back over the same lines in the reverse order. However, they realised that it would be very tedious to do this several times. If BOW were state transparent (that is, if the turtle finished exactly where it started), it would be much more efficient to use BOW for both the drawing and the rubbing out. However, BOW was not state transparent; the turtle finished very, very close to its starting position (the centre of one of the tie's edges) but, on typing PE BOW, the lines were not erased properly.

Dusty's tie was made from two isosceles right-angled triangles. Unaware of Pythagoras' theorem, the children could not anticipate the problem caused by choosing lengths of 20 for the hypotenuse and 15 for each of the other sides. The girls are no wiser now about Pythagoras' theorem than they were at the start, but they do have a much better idea of what is needed to define a triangle. If three angles and one of the sides are determined, then so are the other two sides. None of this was discussed explicitly. The girls used trial and error to try to achieve state transparency. When this failed, they drew the triangles with paper, pencil, ruler and protractor and measured the sides. This was still not accurate enough for the computer, and eventually they decided that it would be easier to use equilateral triangles. Keeping all the sides the same length would avoid the problem altogether. Adapting a problem is one way to set about solving it.

The girls had now managed to draw the tie and to rub it out successfully, but when they repeated the process they learned, to their horror, that the tie did not spin about its centre, as they had expected. It seemed to be quite out of control. The computer was drawing and redrawing the tie in all the wrong places. To make matters worse, each time the lines of the tie were erased, another part of Dusty Bin's face or body disappeared with them. At first the computer's behaviour seemed to be quite irregular and unpredictable. Annabel and Leena almost wanted to give up.

Of course the response of the computer was not erratic at all. It was executing the procedures which it had been taught, and it was doing so with a totally consistent precision. After running their program a few times, the girls noticed that the tie did actually finish in the correct position. Perhaps all was not lost. Further investigation might reveal the source of the problem. The girls did not need to search very far. Once they had decided to examine their work more closely, they realised that the tie was spinning about a point on its edge, and this is why it was moving over a large portion of the screen. It was then fairly straightforward to put the matter right.

Dusty Bin

my Logo Program is called Dusty Bin. It took 2½ months to build. Having every week 2 hours and 20 minutes on the computer. This is what my finsh Program looks like.
This is one of the programs that draws Dusty Bin

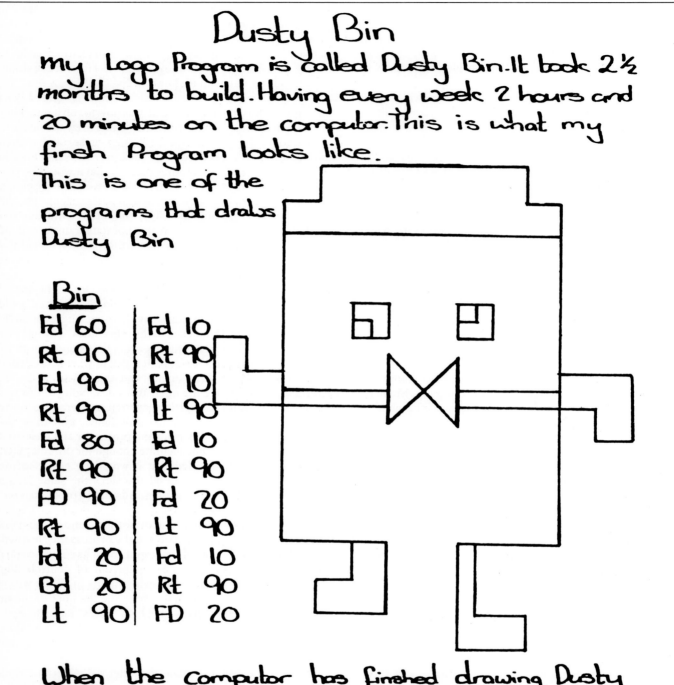

Bin

Fd 60	Fd 10
Rt 90	Rt 90
Fd 90	Fd 10
Rt 90	Lt 90
Fd 80	Fd 10
Rt 90	Rt 90
FD 90	Fd 20
Rt 90	Lt 90
Fd 20	Fd 10
Bd 20	Rt 90
Lt 90	FD 20

When the computer has finshed drawing Dusty Bin it goes to the bowtie and makes it turn around in a circuler direction 9 times and when it has finshed it is in the colour Green

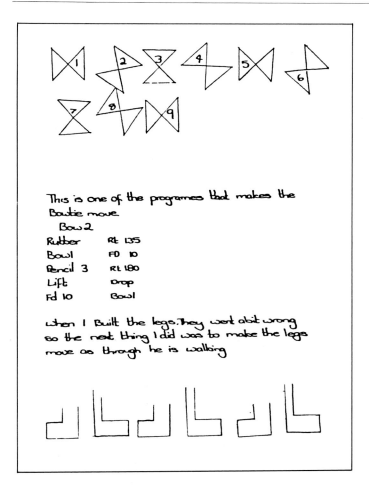

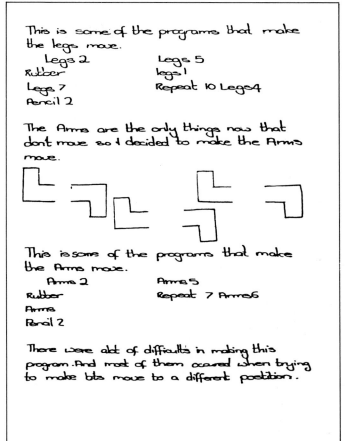

FIGURE 2.19   Details of the procedures used to animate Dusty Bin

All the children in the class came to watch Dusty perform. Working with a network had the advantage that it was easier to encourage the children to learn from one another. Spurred on by Dusty Bin, other children did try to generate movement, but with less success. Linda and Carol had set out with the intention of making the lighthouse flash. They found it too difficult to draw the three rays and then to rub them out repeatedly, but they did create a worthwhile picture (Fig. 2.20).

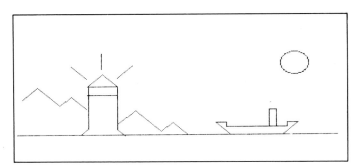

FIGURE 2.20   Example of a picture that resulted from an attempt to produce animation

There were other small projects on movement, which did succeed, and there were also two larger projects to draw a watch and a clock, and these were partially successful.

Katrina and Alison (who drew the watch shown in Fig. 2.21) and Nigel and Daniel all managed to make one hand revolve,

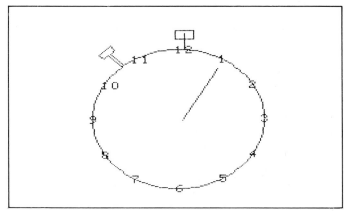

FIGURE 2.21   A watch with a moving hand

but they really wanted to display the two hands moving at different rates. This was not an easy aim for the children, who were all fairly new to Logo at the time. Two university students struggled with the same objective for a long time, and their project will be described in Chapter 6.

Inputs from the keyboard

Moving the turtle around and drawing on the screen is all very well, but it fails to exploit the most exciting aspect of the computer's power. Most computer programs are designed so that they will respond somehow to the people who are using them. When children play computer games, the text and the graphics which are displayed vary according to what the child types at the keyboard (or the way she moves her joystick or her mouse). Like any other programming language, a full version of Logo has the facility to incorporate this feature, and children are highly motivated to work with it. They enjoy writing quizzes and tests and various games.

```
TO QUIZ7
   PRINT [On which bank of the Thames are
      the Houses of Parliament?]
   PRINT [1.South 2.West 3.Lloyds 4.East]
   MAKE "ANSWER RL
   IF :ANSWER = [1] [PRINT "Correct] [WRONG7]
END

TO WRONG7
   PRINT [Wrong, have another go]
   QUIZ7
END
```

This comes from Hazel and Leena's quiz, and there were many other questions (QUIZ1, QUIZ2 etc.) written in similar style.

Sometimes children drew pictures on their screens, which allowed the teacher to suggest an interactive program. Many boys drew stereo sets and televisions, and Clyde and Anil decided to let the user choose which channel to watch. Their program was long, but the relevant portion was as follows:

```
TO QUS
   PRINT [What channel do you want?]
   MAKE "ANS RL
   IF :ANS = [ITV] [ADS]
   IF :ANS = [BBC1] [FOOTBALL]
      .
      .
      .
```

They must have chosen BBC1 before the picture shown in Fig. 2.22 was printed.

Getting an input from the keyboard requires a new technique. We found it very helpful to have a sheet which provided a procedure employing this technique. This allowed the children to leave their projects for a while in order to explore the new idea. When they had mastered it, they could return to their work.

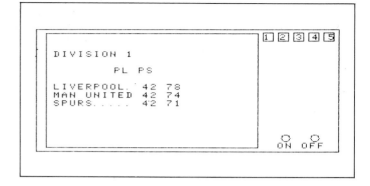

FIGURE 2.22   A picture produced from a procedure with user input

Katrina and Alison had drawn a plate of food with sausages, chips, peas and tomatoes (Fig. 2.23). They had decided early on that they really wanted to provide a menu on the screen, from which the person who was running the program could choose what to eat. When they had finished the drawing, and the time had come to tackle this problem, they left their project and used the sheet to learn the correct technique.

Adding a menu to their program meant that they had to reconsider the procedures they had written. SAUSAGE, TOMATOES, CHIPS and PEAS were a linear sequence of procedures. The turtle's position at the beginning of PEAS was determined by its finishing point in CHIPS. If the girls wanted to allow the user to choose the food, PEAS might have to be called before CHIPS. The procedures needed to be independent.

The ideas for the television project and the dinner menu project developed as the children worked. The teacher made helpful suggestions, and the children took them up when they were ready. The ideas for WORDSEARCH belonged entirely to the children.

Kim and Rupa teamed up with Annabel, and they decided the purpose of their program at the beginning. They started by drawing the grid of letters, with the words which it contained printed at the right-hand side (Fig. 2.24). Then they began all the hard work of allowing the user to locate the various words in the grid. When they had finished some months later, the first question on the screen asked the player whether or not she wanted the rules:

```
TO RULES
   PRINT [Would you like to see the rules? Y/N]
   MAKE "RULE RL
   IF :RULE = [Y] [Y STOP]
   IF :RULE = [N] [N STOP]
   RULES
END
```

This gives you some idea of the sophistication of the girls' work. RULES called itself indefinitely, unless the user typed Y

> ## LOGO REPORT
> ### Meal of the day is ......•
>
> Menu
> 1 Chips
> 2 Sausage
> 3 Tomato
> 4 Peas
>
> When we had drawn our meal we decided to make the computer ask the person what He/She would like for dinner so we made some more programes. In the end what we had was an empty plate on the screen with a question underneath saying "What do you want for Dinner". If the person tuped in "Chips" chips would come up on the plate.

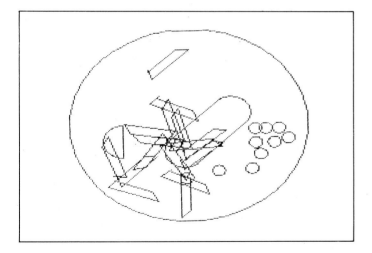

FIGURE 2.23   Another picture which led to a program with user input

```
TO A-Z
   PRINT [Which letters and numbers?]
   MAKE "REPLY RL
   IF :REPLY = [A0-G6] [A0-G6 STOP]
   IF :REPLY = [B2-H2] [B2-H2 STOP]
   .
   .
   .
   A-Z
END
```

A-Z continued to ask the user for her choice until she typed any of the correct answers. When the user entered A0-G6, the computer responded by running the procedure A0-G6, and this drew the line. In fact the line would be drawn regardless of the original choice to locate the word WHISKAS. Maybe one day they will return to their project and put that right. As it was, Kim, Rupa and Annabel were fully justified in feeling very proud of what they had achieved, and they considered the game complete.

Advanced work

The long projects which we have described in detail were done by children who were clearly above average, but the ideas were accessible to many. There were several examples of shorter pieces of work which displayed a similar understanding, if not a similar determination. In this final section we will describe some more advanced programming projects requiring skills which are not widespread.

or N, in which case the program went on to either procedure Y or procedure N. N simply cleared the screen, but Y printed the rules first.

Next the user was asked to type the word of her choice, followed by the positions of the first and the last letters. In the screendump shown in Fig. 2.24 someone must have entered WHISKAS, followed by A0-G6, because the computer responded by drawing a line through that word. The procedure to test for the correct positions was similar in structure to RULES.

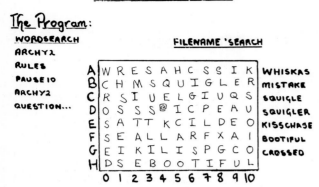

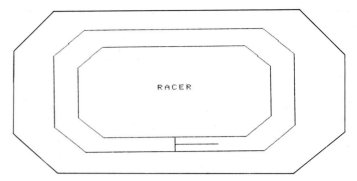

FIGURE 2.25   A racing game in which keyboard input is used to change the car's direction

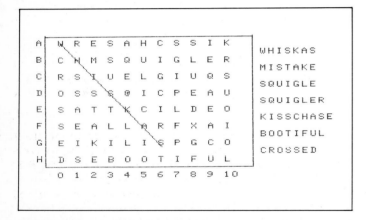

FIGURE 2.24   A wordsearch game which used procedures with input

Many classes these days have one or two children who seem to spend most of their spare time with computers. They are usually boys, and in one of the classes at Trinity School they were both called Daniel. The two Daniels worked apart whenever they could, because they both wanted uninterrupted control of the keyboard, but they were happiest when they had adjacent machines, and they often worked on the same project, each making his own contribution. So it is never absolutely clear who did what, and in the subsequent descriptions we will simply attribute all the work to Daniel.

Daniel's main claim to fame was a game called RACER, which he wrote very early on. This became popular throughout the school, and many children came to the computer room at lunch-time, just to have a go for themselves.

After the track was drawn on the screen, the turtle moved along in a straight line (Fig. 2.25), and the player changed its course by pressing the Z or X key:

```
TO CAR
  IF KEY? [TURNER]
  FD 1
  CAR
END

TO TURNER
  MAKE "K RC
  IF :K = "Z [LT 1]
  IF :K = "X [RT 1]
END
```

KEY? is a test which will be TRUE if someone has pressed any key, and in this case the procedure called TURNER will be executed. In the first line of TURNER, RC (read character) returns the character which has been pressed and stores this as a word. The next two lines test whether the word is "Z or "X, in which case the car-turtle has to be turned. If the player has pressed a different key, and :K is not equal to "Z or "X, then no action is necessary. Daniel needed plenty of help with KEY? and RC, but the design of the procedures is his work.

This idea, which is so neatly expressed, is a powerful one. Spurred on by his many admirers, Daniel subsequently used it wherever he could. The first development was to try to test whether someone's car had crashed. As the program stood, there was no reaction from the computer when the car left the track and wandered all over the screen. The shape of the track made it very difficult to write such a test, and so Daniel experimented with a straight road for a while (Fig. 2.26):

```
TO CAR
  IF KEY? [TURNER]
  IF YCOR > 200 [FLASH STOP]
  IF YCOR < 120 [FLASH STOP]
  FD 1
  CAR
END
```

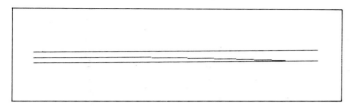

FIGURE 2.26   A linear track used to make it easier to work out when the car has left the track

```
TO FLASH
    REPEAT 5Ø [SETBG 1 SETBG Ø]
END
```

The *y* coordinate of the top of the road was 200 and at the bottom it was 120. If the turtle ventured outside these limits, the screen would flash, and CAR would stop, ending the program.

This version was not as popular as Daniel's original because the track was less interesting and there was not actually very much for the players to do. Consequently, Daniel decided to leave the idea for a while, but he returned to it some months later. He was attracted by the possibility of having two cars racing around his original track (Fig. 2.27), and his teacher helped by supplying a procedure which made the turtle swap from one location, which it had to store, to the other, which it had stored previously:

```
TO SWAP
    MAKE "TEMPSTORE SE HEADING POS
    SETH FIRST :STORE
    SETPOS BF :STORE
    MAKE "STORE :TEMPSTORE
END
```

The task which remained for Daniel after being provided with SWAP was not insignificant. He had to incorporate it into his program, so that it was called only when the player whose car was not moving pressed a key. He also had to initialise STORE. At first he did not realise this, and when Logo complained that there was no name "STORE, Daniel was forced to look inside SWAP and to find out what was going on. As he explored, he made the procedure his own by adding one or two trivial lines, and he learned a lot this way. SWAP was not presented to him as a black box; it was a glass box, which was there to be studied.

The result of all this was a two-car race in which each player had two different keys to manipulate her own car. Having the turtle swap from one car to another was a slow business, but the children did not mind too much. Sprites would have been much faster, but with sprites there would not have been very much there for Daniel to do himself.

There were two further major developments of RACER. One was another race, between two horses this time (Fig. 2.28). The horses were not controlled by the players, but there

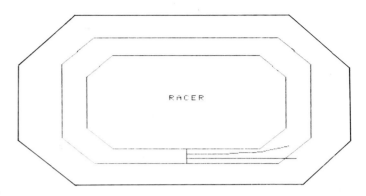

FIGURE 2.27   A version of the racing game with two cars

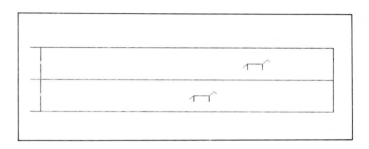

FIGURE 2.28   Another version of the racing game with two horses: the speeds were affected by random numbers

was a random element built into their speeds, and the players were invited to place their bets at the beginning. The other project stemming from RACER was a sketch-pad program. The hidden turtle moved along, leaving a trace, and the operator could control the direction of the turtle, the colour of its ink and its speed.

Another theme to which Daniel often returned during his course was that of mazes (Fig. 2.29). Daniel wrote 15 procedures just to draw the maze on the screen. There was no regularity in the drawing, and so each part of the maze had to be designed individually. Movement through the maze was generated as in RACER, but the player could choose the speed at the start (:S), and pressing Z or X turned the path through an angle of 90°. Also, no trace of the path remained, even though the movement was visible:

```
TO FOR
    PD FD :S
    PE BK :S FD :S
END
```

The main new feature of this project was that it included a test for the position of the turtle. If the player managed to reach a certain area of the maze, she needed to be told that she had won.

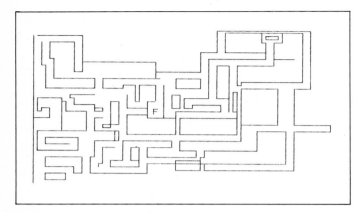

FIGURE 2.29   A maze produced using some of the concepts of the racing game

```
TO TEST
    IF (AND XCOR < 36 YCOR < 15 XCOR > −84
        YCOR > −45) [WIN]
END
```

TEST was included in the recursive procedure which made the turtle move, and so it was called continually.

At a later date, Daniel went on to design a maze program in which the player could only see a small part of the maze on the screen at any one time. For instance, a large T-junction might appear on the screen, with the prompt 'SOUTH, EAST or WEST?'. On typing S, E or W, the screen was cleared, and another part of the maze appeared. This was achieved by planning the maze on a coordinate grid and having the computer keep a check of the position on this grid.

Long projects

Many of the children undertook long projects like Menu, Racer and Dusty Bin. These projects often had common features as far as the learning style was concerned. The children chose their own topics, and they decided whether or not to pursue their projects. Many successful ventures seem to contain three distinct stages.

Firstly there is a *gestation* period, in which the children become committed to an idea and make it their own. This is characterised by work which is relatively low level. Katrina and Alison had only been learning Logo for a little while, and they needed to spend time drawing their plate of food before they were ready to tackle the difficulties of an interactive program. Their teacher had suggested the idea quite early on, and although they appeared to ignore the intervention at the time, they did take it up later, when they were ready. They needed the opportunity to gather their thoughts, to contemplate the new idea and to make it their own.

Seeing them at work during this gestation stage, a sceptical person may have pointed out that drawing the chips was not at all difficult, and she may have wondered just how long the children had been 'messing about'. But the time spent was important. The children were contemplating the abstract ideas required to add a menu to their program.

The same thing was true with Dusty Bin. In fact it was quite a surprise when Annabel and Leena suddenly announced that they intended to make the tie spin. It probably was not a sudden decision, however. They had been spending some time drawing Dusty on the screen. They were not being stretched at this stage, but they were preparing themselves for the struggle to follow. In Wordsearch the children also knew their objectives from the start, but they spent time initially drawing the grid of letters on the screen.

The *innovation* stage of a project is the most exciting period of time, and it is often the shortest of the three stages. It is the climax of the project, when there are many struggles and progress is not smooth. This particular stage is usually the most exciting for the teacher because the children's learning is transparent. More conventional teaching often attempts to capture the innovation stage while avoiding the other two. This means that the knowledge is not in any meaningful context for the children, and there will be resistance to hard thinking. With less time available, it would have been quite understandable for the teacher to suggest that the children should try to simulate movement, say, without any context. This may have achieved some successes, but many children would only experience the frustration that is so often associated with failure at school. When the gestation phase of a project has been allowed to take its natural course, the children enter the innovation stage with a positive attitude.

Finally, there is a period of *consolidation*, which happens naturally when the children are given freedom and time. Having achieved their main goals, the program is enlarged without the development of anything new. Katrina and Alison simply added more choice to their menu. Annabel and Leena made Dusty's arms and legs move. Practice is an important element in the learning process and, when it is self-imposed, children will consolidate their knowledge effectively. This final stage is also a natural way for the children to wind down and to accept the end of the project which they have created and which belongs to them.

Not all the children's work was in the form of a project, although we obviously encouraged this approach. At the beginning of this chapter we described how children would explore in a fairly random way in order to understand new ideas. This continued to some extent all the way through their course. One or two children worked for more than a year without ever settling down to one long project. Apart from the exploration of new commands and new techniques, such as recursion, children often picked up an idea which they worked at for the course of a single lesson. Posters on the classroom walls suggested patterns that children wanted to design, and the handbook which was available provided another source of ideas.

When children tried to copy a particular poster, their work was goal directed, and this required a discipline which is an important feature of learning to program. Within their own projects the children often lost sight of, or changed, their goal. They were at liberty to draw a flat roof on their house if a pointed roof became too difficult to manage. After some time it was no bad thing for them to have to draw precisely what the poster depicted.

As in all areas of education, the best results are obtained when the learning style is balanced. Children need to spend some time exploring, and they also need to tackle goal-directed tasks, and we found that this balance was achieved more readily when the children were working on their own projects. The long-term projects generated the need for short explorations and also for goal-directed tasks. When the children needed a new technique, they would leave their project for a while to explore, and there would always be some tasks thrown up by a project which the children had to tackle directly.

Those who spent every lesson doing something different were much more likely to lose interest, because they had no sense of purpose. It became increasingly difficult to persuade these few individuals to work on a long-term goal, and they never felt the same pride that the owners of a complex program displayed when their work was admired by the other children in the class. They never had the satisfaction of having achieved something really worthwhile.

3 Turtles and Early Programming

Turtle geometry

Children could start their Logo programming by working within any one of a number of different microworlds. A range of activities was described in Chapter 1 of this book. Idris and Pindhi were given the procedure called NOTE so that they were free to explore the effect of stringing different sequences of notes together. They typed NOTE "A 10 to get an A for a short duration and then NOTE "C 150 to get a longer C. Rebecca and Alison might have started their Logo by moving the various parts of a crane. However, the most popular starting point in schools today is certainly turtle geometry. This is partly due to the fact that the turtle was available before the other microworlds. (In fact it was available before Logo.) But there are two more important reasons, which are to do with the nature of turtle geometry itself.

First of all the turtle is body syntonic. This means that its movements are in harmony with our own. The sorts of instructions which the turtle requires are similar to those we might use to direct someone to the station . . . go 200 yards along this street, take the second on your right, and it's about 100 yards on the left-hand side. Secondly, children, and especially younger children, can derive enormous benefits from working in direct drive with a turtle. This means that they can do a lot of work before they have learned how to write procedures without actually programming. This is because the effects of turtle commands are lasting. When a child types FD 100, the turtle will move so that it is in a different place when it has executed the command. If the pen is down, a line will be drawn. In contrast, within a music microworld a sound is heard, and then it is lost. It is more difficult to make progress unless the children are able to string commands together and to write procedures.

Turtle geometry could involve children with a floor turtle, or it might be with the screen turtle alone. Before we discuss some of the implications of the different sorts of turtles, we will consider the conceptual activity of playing turtle.

Playing turtle

Playing turtle is not an alternative to floor turtles or screen turtles. All Logo learners will find that they need to play turtle at some times, whatever the form of the actual turtle they are using. Children who have learned to write procedures are often challenging themselves to write them without testing them in direct drive first. This is quite healthy, but it is to be expected that they will make mistakes sometimes. They may have written 10 or 12 commands: FD 50, RT 90, FD 100, LT 45 etc. When they test their procedure by typing its name, the turtle may draw something quite unexpected. There may only be one small bug. Perhaps one of the commands should have been LT 45 and not RT 45. But the bug will not be obvious. The drawing might look so wrong that the children think there are several bugs. If children ask for their teacher's help in these sorts of circumstances, the best advice she can offer them is to play turtle. The children should leave their computer, write the list of commands on paper, and actually trace the turtle's path by walking around the classroom. It is very likely that this will shed light on the source of the error, and the children can then begin to de-bug their procedure.

Playing turtle is so important for the full control of the turtle's path that it is worth devoting time for class activities. Children can work in pairs with one child, the turtle, blind-folded, while her partner, the computer, has to issue the commands (Fig. 3.1). Indeed, this is one way to introduce Logo to children, in which case the children could develop the vocabulary of FD, BK, LT and RT for themselves. We have found that the children start by walking around the room together, one child issuing commands as and when it seems to be appropriate . . . go forward a little . . . now stop . . . turn left . . . forward again . . . stop . . . . If she cannot articulate her commands very well, the child who is playing the computer often holds onto the turtle-child physically. We needed to explain that the computer should not keep 'stopping' the turtle, and under no circumstances should she touch her. She should issue commands one by one, and these should be obeyed by the turtle without interruption. A class discussion on this matter led to the suggestion that, when the computer instructs the turtle to move forwards, she also has to say how far.

A similar class discussion might be used to establish the need to quantify the turns. Without the teacher's intervention, the children are likely to restrict themselves to the instructions 'turn left' or 'turn right'. After all, it is possible to reach any desired position using only turns of 90°. Perhaps the teacher would need to introduce the notion of economy to give some purpose to the use of other angles. 'What is the quickest way to instruct your turtle to move from here to here?' Of course, the teacher needs to consider the children's understanding of angle before she decides how much to pursue this idea.

FIGURE 3.1   Children with blind-folds playing turtle

Once the children are able to issue appropriate commands, one at a time, the teacher might lead on to the idea of a procedure. At this stage, she may want to get the children to write sequences of commands without necessarily referring to procedures explicitly. This could be achieved by getting the computers to navigate their turtles through a maze. Perhaps each pair of children could now join another pair, to form groups of four. Each group could design a small maze for themselves using three or four chairs and some books. The children would then revert to their original pairs to write their sequences of commands, and the other pair in each group of four could test them.

The floor turtle[1]

We said earlier that children identify with the turtle, but this will be achieved far more readily with a floor turtle than it is with an arrowhead on the screen. Children will stand behind the floor turtle as it moves, and they learn to choose the correct command by putting themselves in the turtle's place (Fig. 3.2). After having played turtle, it is a natural progression to work with a floor turtle. A screen turtle is more abstract. When it is pointing downwards, it is often difficult for children to decide which sort of turn is needed to make it point towards, say, the bottom left-hand corner of the screen. It has been suggested

that the monitor could be turned so that the screen becomes horizontal, and the children are able to look down on it from above. This might help, but it is not very practical, and it would still not be the same as a real object which moves about in the classroom.

The floor turtle is also important for the many children whose concept of angle is not complete. When a child gives the computer the command RT 3Ø, the effect on the floor turtle is obvious. The robot turns, slowly and deliberately, in a clockwise direction. The behaviour of the screen turtle is different. There is a flicker on the screen, and the direction of the arrowhead changes. The child has to assume that the turtle rotates, since no movement is apparent. The turtle disappears and then reappears instantaneously with a new orientation. If the command given to the turtle is RT 36Ø, there is no visible effect on the screen, whereas the floor turtle dutifully executes a complete turn before coming to rest in the same place and with its original heading.

Another major advantage of the floor turtle, particularly for younger children, is that it can be used for numerous activities before a pen is introduced. Children may find drawing difficult if they are not yet able to control the turtle with any degree of accuracy. A floor turtle without a pen can be used to knock over a paper cup on the floor or to navigate a more complex route. It can be used with a ping-pong ball to play turtle football. It is true that a piece of Blu-Tack could be placed on the screen

FIGURE 3.2   Children working with a floor turtle

monitor with the aim of trying to get the turtle to the Blu-Tack, or the turtle's route might be drawn on a transparent overlay, which could be taped to the screen. But these activities do not seem very natural. The screen turtle always starts with its pen down, and so the children are plunged into drawing before they may be ready for it.

But what about the practicalities of floor turtles? If you intend to buy one, the main choice that you will have to make is whether you want it to be remote controlled. The obvious advantage of this is the fact that there is no flex to get tangled or for the children to trip over. However, it could be that infants are more likely to understand the turtle's connection with the computer if there is a tangible link. A remote-controlled turtle will be able to travel further away from the computer than its conventional counterpart, but if it strays behind something too solid it will not be able to 'hear' its instructions. Its main disadvantage, however, is that, if it is in use for much of the day, it will need to be re-charged every night.

Should you buy a turtle? It has to be reported that in the school where we learned most of our Logo there were three accidents within the first half-term. The first one happened when the most timid of all the children got out of his seat and kicked the poor creature. A hair-line fracture in the skull was diagnosed. The second incident, however, was more serious. A sturdy, male, six-foot teacher simply walked all over it. This time it was a brain haemorrhage. The school technician was

not sure whether to laugh or cry as he took it off to his surgery for a thick metal plate to be implanted. The turtle recovered again, but the third accident was almost fatal. The turtle was knocked off a table and its skull had to be replaced.

Nevertheless, if you can afford a turtle, you should probably buy one. In ideal circumstances many secondary school children, and most primary school children, should have access to a floor turtle for much of the time. In practice this is rarely the case. Quite apart from the difficulties described above, turtles are expensive. However, you may be able to borrow one from a local teachers' centre. Although it may not always be possible for children to use one continually, all children who learn Logo should at least see one being demonstrated.

Programmable toys

Many primary schools have programmable toys, such as Bigtrak or George (Fig. 3.3), which can be used for preliminary activities before children move on to floor turtles or screen turtles. Sadly, these particular toys are not being made any longer, but there are plenty lurking at the back of toy cupboards, which enthusiastic advertising will usually uncover. There may also be new toys on the market[2] which can be used

FIGURE 3.3   Bigtrak and George

as a cheaper alternative to a floor turtle. However, there are some important aspects in which they may differ. Firstly, the toys might not be able to be used for drawing if there is nowhere to insert a pen. They are also far less accurate than floor turtles, particularly in turning, and their accuracy often depends on the surface they are running on. This can be a little frustrating at times, but it is not too serious since accuracy is generally more important for drawing than it is for other activities. In fact the inaccuracy can stimulate a lot of interesting problem solving.

A serious drawback with both Bigtrak and George is that they can only be programmed to remember one sequence of commands. This means that children will not appreciate the value of procedures. But many valuable early programming activities are possible with these toys, and starting with one of them is certainly better for younger children than using the screen turtle straight away. We regret the choice of a militaristic appearance for Bigtrak, and of a boy's name for George, but both of these can be altered.

The transition to the screen

It is difficult to say how much time children need with the floor turtle before they are ready to graduate to the screen. Clearly, older children need less time than younger ones. For many children in secondary schools, it may be sufficient for them only to see a floor turtle being used in the same room occasionally. Primary school children who have always used the floor turtle may become frustrated with its lack of speed. If they want to start drawing patterns with many lines, they may make their own decision to reject the floor turtle. In this case the children will have seen the patterns forming on the screen whilst they were concentrating on the floor turtle, and so the transition will be natural and smooth.

Children with less personal experience with the floor turtle will often need to be reminded about the relationship between the two animals. As they look at the arrowhead on the screen, they will need to be told to imagine that they are a fly on the ceiling, looking down on the turtle, which is crawling about on the floor. The children may have played computer games in which the direction of movement is controlled by commands which refer to the monitor screen. Key presses or a joystick will have been used to move 'up' or 'down' or towards the left or the right of the screen. Turtle geometry, however, is different. The commands refer to the turtle's position and heading, and the shape of the screen is quite irrelevant. When children ask how to move the turtle 'upwards', they need to be reminded about the floor turtle.

There is not very much to say about screen turtles themselves. If you look at several different versions of Logo you will notice th̄ ̄ ̄ ̄ape of the turtle varies a little. Some turtles look likε ̱urtles, and others are simple arrowheads. The quality of the drawing on the screen also varies, but this is totally dependent on the computer rather than the Logo. Fundamentally, all screen turtles behave in the same way. However, there are turtle graphics packages on the market which drive turtles but which are not Logo.

Turtle graphics packages

We explained in the Introduction that there are differences between the various versions of Logo (LCSI, MIT and RML) and, while some of these differences have profound implications for the advanced programmer, they need not concern most teachers or most children. However, the differences between a turtle graphics package like DART[3] or ARROW[4] and a full implementation of the Logo language are worth knowing about. In the remainder of this section we will refer simply to DART, probably the most popular turtle graphics package, and Logo.

DART was available for the BBC micro before Logo, and in the DART handbook it states that it should be destroyed when Logo does arrive. Comparing DART with Logo, it is inevitable that DART will come under heavy attack, but it is important to stress that DART is an excellent piece of educational software, and many teachers use it to the advantage of their pupils. The relationship between DART and Logo is similar to the one between programmable toys and floor turtles. DART has no educational advantage over Logo, but at present it is much cheaper and is a very good second best. DART can be used to drive a floor turtle as well as a screen turtle, and so it might provide a satisfactory, economic, alternative for younger children, who will easily be able to transfer to Logo later on.

So what are the differences? Firstly, it is obvious that DART cannot be used for other microworlds, such as music and the control of machines, which do not depend upon the turtle. Logo is a general programming language, like Basic or Pascal, whereas DART is restricted to drawing pictures and patterns with a turtle. Much of the educational software which is used in schools could be written in Logo, but not in DART. When children are encouraged to develop their own projects, one favourite choice is to create a quiz. This could not be done with DART because it offers no facility for getting an input from the keyboard. In other words, the computer cannot ask the user a question with DART.

Another important feature which is missing from DART is the word IF. With Logo, as with all other programming languages, the programmer is able to get her program to make decisions. For instance, if she is drawing a wallpaper pattern, her procedure for a row of flowers may contain the following command: IF the next flower goes over the edge of the screen, then stop, otherwise continue to draw another flower. There are no facilities at all within DART for dealing with lists or any text. Data cannot be stored and words cannot be printed on the screen. There are other deficie̱ ̄ ̄ ̄̀ could be mentioned when DART is being ̱ ̄ ̄ ̄ with Logo, but to describe them all would becoṁε too technical. The important point is that, given time, plenty of children, primary school children as well as secondary, will outgrow DART. No more than one or two computer addicts in the sixth form will ever outgrow Logo.

Procedures

When a child types a command, say FD 100, at top-level, she is not programming yet. She is working in 'direct drive'. Her instruction will be obeyed and the turtle will move forwards, but nothing will be stored in the computer's memory. In Logo, programming starts with writing procedures, and this is a very important stage in the learning process. The concept of a procedure is powerful, and there are many different ways in which it can be understood. In this section we will explore some of these, and we will also discuss some of the technical problems which many children encounter.

Children are rarely resistant to the use of procedures, and the concept is an accessible one. They enjoy the power of being able to instruct the computer to execute a long routine by typing a single command. The children may have struggled for many hours, and written several lines of code, to produce a drawing. Imagine their delight as they type one word at the keyboard, and the complete picture develops for everyone to see.

When we learn something new, it can often be helpful to give it a name. To write a procedure is to name a sequence of commands. The procedures available to a programmer are the words of her language and, when she writes a new procedure, she has created a new word. If her procedure is called BOAT, this new word can then be used in exactly the same sort of way as any of the primitive words, such as FD or REPEAT. The difference is that the programmer had to teach the computer what BOAT means. She had to explain how it works by defining it in terms of a sequence of other words, in much the same way as a dictionary defines the words of a natural language. The definition is not fixed, but it can be altered by the programmer. The idea of teaching the computer a new word is a powerful one, and it is useful for teachers to refer to it explicitly when children are learning about procedures. A new procedure that has been created can be used to define further procedures, and this idea will be examined more fully later in the book.

Saving work

Children who are working with a floor turtle can be encouraged to stay with the same objective, and to continue their work from one lesson to the next, simply by keeping their drawing safely. When the turtle is just an image on the screen, their drawings will disappear when the machine is turned off. Children are often half way through their pictures when they are forced to clear away. If they are working in direct drive, without writing procedures, they will need to type all their commands again in order to continue with their work. Indeed, many children are first introduced to procedures because they want some way to save what they are doing. Of course, Logo procedures do much more than allow the programmer's work to be saved on a disc, but it is important that children can see a reason for the acquisition of a new idea. Providing them with a way to save their work allows the teacher to introduce procedures whenever it is appropriate for any particular group of children.

The main difficulty with this approach is that the children will need to master the technicalities of writing procedures and of saving them on a disc in quick succession. It would be useful for the teacher to have prepared some duplicated sheets which show clearly the syntax of the commands for the two processes. Nevertheless, children may still become confused. A child may have saved a copy of her procedures on disc during the course of a lesson and then subsequently changed some of them. The new versions of her procedures are stored in the computer's memory, but the disc still has the old copies. When the lesson finishes, the child may not realise that she has to save copies of the amended procedures if she wants to retrieve them in the following lesson. In order to prevent this confusion, the teacher will need to distinguish carefully between the two sorts of memory. She must explain to the children that the computer's memory is short term. When the machine is switched off, it will forget everything it knows. A disc, in contrast, is for long-term storage. Some teachers find it helpful to compare the computer's memory to the human brain and the disc to a piece of paper. This metaphor allows them to stress that it is not the procedures themselves which are being saved on the disc, but copies of the procedures.

In LCSI and MIT Logo the word SAVE has to be followed by another word, which will become the name of the file on the disc. It is good practice to use a filename which either identifies the project or the children who own the work. For instance, if Anne and Josephine wanted to save all the procedures which were in the memory of their computer, they could type SAVE "ANNJO. At the beginning of the following lesson, they would type LOAD "ANNJO to retrieve their work from the disc. At the end, if they had written some more procedures, they could type SAVE "ANNJO2. It is probably worth suggesting this idea fairly forcefully, otherwise the children may use procedure names for their files, and this will add to their confusion. It may even be worth introducing SAVE by showing the children its full form, in which specified procedures are saved. A child called Idris who had written five procedures, but only wanted to save BOAT and SEA, could type SAVE "IDRIS [BOAT SEA]. Insisting on this form may help the children to distinguish between the file on the disc and the procedures in the computer's memory.

Editing procedures

Children can easily change their procedures when there is a bug. All versions of Logo provide a full-screen editor, which behaves like a simple word processor. It can be used to edit procedures by changing or removing existing commands or by adding new ones. Some children might have one or two technical problems when they first use the editor, but they are not usually too serious. A common early difficulty is with the delete key. Children who want to remove a letter may position the cursor on top of it and then press the key, only to find that the wrong letter has been deleted. In fact the cursor should be placed immediately to the right of the offending character, since the delete key will erase the character to its left.

With LCSI versions of Logo, procedures can be written using the command TO, which does not invoke the editor. Its main benefit is that the children will not lose the picture on the screen. On all the popular school micros except the RML 380Z and 480Z machines, using the editor will destroy the picture. However, in practice, children will need to edit very soon after they have learned about procedures themselves, and so TO is probably redundant. When TO is being used, children often want to change something, after a typing error or another obvious mistake, and the only advice to offer them is to END the process of writing the procedure and to use the editor. It is perfectly legitimate to edit a procedure before it has been written, and so some teachers might prefer not to introduce the children to TO but to use EDIT from the start.

While defining a procedure with TO, the prompt at the left-hand side of the screen changes, usually from a question mark (?) to a sideways V (>). This is to remind the programmer that she is not at top-level. She cannot now type any instructions and expect them to be obeyed immediately. Whatever she does type will become part of the definition of her new procedure. The only way to retrieve the question mark is to type END and thereby to finish the defining process. This often seems to cause some confusion amongst the children, who may take some time to accept that the turtle does not move while they are defining procedures. It may be that they just forget to type END, or sometimes they type it on the same line as another command, whereas END has to be the last line, on its own. Whatever the reason, we often see children furiously typing all sorts of commands, and getting more and more frustrated when the computer seems to be ignoring them.

The fact that the only difference on the screen is the small prompt cannot be the only reason for this confusion, because the same thing happens within the editor. Invoking the editor causes the whole screen to change, yet many children still often forget where they are. It is not uncommon to see a child type the name of the procedure, after she has finished defining it, while she is still using the editor. She was, of course, trying to execute the procedure, but to do that she needed to be back at top-level, with the question mark for her prompt. When nothing is drawn, some children immediately realise their mistake, and subsequently they escape from the editor. Their procedure now has its title as the last instruction, and the children are accidentally introduced to recursion.

In general, children have to understand about the different modes of Logo. When they are using TO, they are in teaching mode, and all they can do is teach; when they are within the editor, they can only edit or teach; and when they are at top-level, their instructions will be obeyed immediately.

4 The Teacher's Role

It may seem strange, and perhaps impertinent, to include a chapter on the teacher's role in a book which we hope will be read by many experienced teachers. We have included it because we know that working with Logo has forced us to reconsider many of our existing ideas about teaching and about relationships between pupils and teachers.

Logo was designed to be a language for learning. With Logo, children can take responsibility for what and how they learn. At first, many people interpreted this as an extreme form of discovery learning. They thought that it was the teacher's job to set up the machinery and, from then on, the learning would take care of itself. A bit of occasional maintenance was all that would be required, and on no account should the teacher actually tell a child anything.

It is not difficult to see why this view prevailed, and to some extent still does. The philosophy of Logo is a child-centred one. It emphasises learning much more than teaching. Children are often working on their own projects, and teachers are advised to consider their interventions carefully. But this does not imply that teachers should not intervene at all, or that the teacher is unimportant in a Logo classroom. On the contrary, we feel that the teacher's role is vital, and that it involves teaching and not just managing the classroom. It is often appropriate to give information or to suggest a particular action for some children. Different approaches will suit different situations, so what follows will not attempt to suggest hard-and-fast rules.

A theme which will run through much of this chapter is that of control. Traditionally, teachers have control over almost everything that happens in classrooms, from deciding what is learnt, and in what order, to organising seating arrangements and rationing paper and pencils. Using Logo provides an opportunity to encourage children to take responsibility for their learning. Handing over, and accepting, control can be difficult for teachers and pupils, and in this chapter we shall be highlighting some of the special features of the teacher's role in a Logo classroom which can help this process. Some of these features may already be part of your teaching style; others may be less familiar to you. In the first part of the chapter we will look at organisational issues, and later we will consider interaction with children.

Lesson format

Organising lessons in which children are working on Logo, or indeed other activities at the computer, may involve making considerable changes to the normal routine. This will be equally true whether the lesson is in a computer room, where all the children are able to use the machines at once, or when one or two machines are in use in an ordinary classroom. Clearly, using Logo is not compatible with class teaching, but fits naturally into a situation where children are working in groups, either in a mathematics lesson or in an integrated session in a primary school classroom. Handling a lesson where groups of children are working in this way does present quite different problems to those of talking to the whole class, and this may be unfamiliar to some teachers.

We found that there was a danger of getting caught up with the problems of one group at the beginning of the lesson, so that other groups did not settle down properly. It is helpful to make a deliberate effort to deal only with immediate problems in, say, the first ten minutes of a lesson, until all the groups are settled and able to get on. Often the initial problems in any particular lesson will be technical ones which can be dealt with quite quickly without absorbing too much of the teacher's attention. This is important in order to establish a good working atmosphere which will later allow the teacher to spend longer periods giving more concentrated attention to groups who need her help and advice. We also found that we needed to talk explicitly to children about being aware of when we were involved in a discussion with a particular group, so that they did not interrupt as soon as they came across a problem. As the children became more experienced, they realised that they could solve many of their problems without our help by talking to other children or using the handbook.

Hardware

One obvious aspect of the teacher's role which worries many teachers when they first begin working with Logo is that of managing the hardware; the computers, disc drives, floor turtle, printer etc. It is quite natural for teachers who are unfamiliar with the machinery to be nervous, and it is important that they allow themselves enough time to become confident. It also helps to show the children how to use all the facilities that they will need, so that the teacher does not have to take all the responsibility for handling them.

Children will need time to get over the novelty of using the computer and other machines too, particularly when they are also getting used to having the freedom to choose what they work on. One novelty that children in our classes needed time to get used to was the printer. The printer is a valuable device to have in the classroom and we often encouraged the pupils to print out their procedures, so that they could study more than they were able to display on the screen at any one moment. At first, whenever we suggested this, the printer was already occupied by other groups using it to get (several) copies of their pictures. It is perfectly reasonable for children to want to take away a printed copy of a screen picture they have designed, but this is very time consuming. It was tempting to limit this particular use of the machine, but there was plenty of time available, and we allowed things to progress more naturally. Gradually the children tired of printing out everything, and they learned to discriminate.

Room layout

In our description of Bridgeton School, we were trying to give the impression of a school in which computers were taken for granted in the same way as other equipment. If children are to get the most out of working with computers, it is important that they are not seen as something separate and special. The computers will be integrated much more easily if the machines are put into ordinary classrooms rather than being kept in a special area. The informal arrangement of furniture in most primary school classrooms makes it much easier to include computers unobtrusively than the more formal rows usually seen in secondary schools. It is important to arrange things so that it is convenient for the teacher to sit with a group working at the machine and for other children to have the opportunity to be aware of what is going on. If there is more than one computer in the room, it is useful to have the flexibility to have them close together or separated, according to the kind of work that the children are doing.

Time

If there are one or two computers in the classroom, rather than children having to go to a special computer room to use them, the teacher will need to organise how the time at the computer is to be shared amongst the class. Logo offers the opportunity for learning to take place in a natural way but, if this is to happen, there must be enough time for children to create, develop and become the owners of their projects. This needs to be balanced against maintaining children's interest between their turns at the machine. There will, of course, be constraints in terms of the time-tabling of lessons and access to computers. These will be different in primary and secondary schools, and they will also differ greatly between individual schools.

Involving the children in the organisation of a time-sharing rota is another way in which a teacher can encourage them to take control of the situation. The amount of time each group can have at the computer may be governed by the length of a particular lesson but, if it is possible to allow more flexibility, this can be valuable. Inevitably there will be some children who will monopolise the machines if they are allowed to, but they are really the exceptions. Once they have got over the novelty, most children will get a feeling for when they have completed the productive work that they can do in one session. This will not happen overnight and it will need a lot of reinforcement from the teacher, who at first may need to suggest strongly when a suitable stopping point has come. A rota with a strict time-table may seem less trouble, but it will not help the children to develop a sense of responsibility.

With a group of older children who had done quite a lot of work in Logo we used a rota system to allow them to combine Logo with their other work in mathematics without making an artificial break between the two. In each lesson, the rota showed which children had first priority for the use of the two computers in the room. If they did not want to do Logo in that lesson because they were in the middle of some other work, they could relinquish their turn, but they could not be sure of having another chance to use the computer until it was their turn again.

Some system of recording whose turn is next which the children can operate themselves will also help a time-sharing system to work smoothly. A colleague working with infant children uses a shoe box which stands by the computer, holding a card for each group of children. The card contains the children's names and a record of the dates of their computer sessions and the file names they use to store their work. When the group's card comes to the front of the box, they take their turn, and they replace the card at the back of the box when they have finished.

Partnerships

Working cooperatively is an important aspect of Logo. Quite apart from the practicalities of not having enough machines available for everyone to work on their own, the advantages of working with a partner are enormous. Discussing ideas is an important part of any learning. Putting your thoughts into words is a valuable way of clarifying them for yourself. The experience of starting to explain something, only to realise that you have not really understood it yourself, is a common one. Thinking aloud can be a powerful way of exposing your own misunderstandings, and it also provides a means of sorting out the confusions by talking them through. This acitivity is much less threatening, and more meaningful, when the person you are talking to is a fellow pupil, who you know does not already understand what you are trying to explain, rather than a teacher, who you think already knows all the answers. Sharing ideas gives the opportunity to learn from others and to see many different views of a problem.

When children are working in Logo, it is natural for them to discuss work with their partner, but forming stable working partnerships is not something that all children take to naturally. In our classrooms, we have found that girls seem to be more comfortable with cooperative working than many boys. Typically, the girls formed more stable partnerships, while the boys tended to change partners more often and were often keen to work on their own. Some of our lessons were in a computer room in which children worked on a network. To begin with, these lessons would often start with several boys rushing in and sitting one to a machine, while the girls waited patiently with their partners. We inevitably told the children without partners to sit away from the machines, so that those who were ready could begin.

One way to overcome this problem would be for the teacher to determine the children's partnerships herself, but this would be missing an opportunity to encourage the children to take control. We allowed time for the children to choose their own partners and to change these as they needed to. We also took every opportunity to get over the message implicitly that working with a partner is useful and important, and occasionally we talked more explicitly to children who were having difficulty in settling into partnerships.

Inevitably, there will be some children who prefer to work on their own at some times, particularly as they become more experienced programmers, and it is reasonable for a teacher to respect this. As this puts additional pressure on machine time, children who want to work alone may have to balance this by having less time in lessons; they may be encouraged to use their break times to continue working on their projects. In some of our classes, when plenty of machines were available, pairs of children who were experienced programmers liked to work on their own, but sitting near enough to one another to look over at each other's screens. Although they were working on separate projects, they discussed their work and offered each other help and advice.

Encouraging a Logo environment

Everything that children do in Logo is to some extent public: you cannot cover up a screen in the same way that many children hide their written work from each other. It is easy and natural for children to look at, and to comment on, each other's projects, and so to learn from each other. The teacher can encourage this further by giving space for wall displays of children's work and other stimulus material. The relationships between the children are different from those in a more conventional classroom. They tend to share ideas and knowledge in an environment which does not continually stress competition.

If the children are permitted to use the computers for Logo during breaks and lunch hours, there are still further benefits. Children from different classes will have different approaches to the work. They will have learned different things and communication between them will be valuable. This is possible since a good microworld is of interest at various stages of the children's development. The common environment will allow the younger children to learn from the older ones.

For some teachers, the thought of children having access to each other's work in this way may raise the problem of copying. A certain amount of copying, and the right sort of copying, is perfectly healthy. Encouraging children to learn from each other is, in a sense, encouraging them to copy. Some children in our classes learned about variables by copying a program directly from a wall display. Children often copy something

that looks attractive, and then they make it their own by adding to it or changing it.

Too much copying is unhealthy and it militates against children getting involved in their own projects. As with using the printer, children can learn to be more discriminating in the way that they use each other's ideas and procedures, provided that they have the time, and the guidance, to do this constructively. The teacher's first instinct may be to try to impose her own rules about copying, but this will not necessarily achieve the result of helping the children to develop a responsible attitude. Probably the children will still copy, but they will become more devious and they will copy in less obvious ways.

Resources

Every classroom, whatever the age of the children and whatever subject is being taught, should be well-stocked with resources. With Logo there is a constant interaction between the children and their computers, and in this chapter we are also highlighting the benefits of discussion between the teacher and children and between the children themselves. Children also need to be stimulated by books, work-cards and posters, but there are obvious dangers here. It is too easy for children to become dependent on textual resources, so that when they have finished a task they do not have the initiative to develop further ideas of their own. In this section we will describe some of the resources which we have used, but we will also try to express some of our reservations.

We produced our own Logo handbook because we did not feel that the manual provided was accessible to the children (are they ever?). This was important since we wanted the children to be able to answer some of their own questions independently. Some manuals start with a tutorial section, which the children need to work through, step by step, but we certainly did not want to provide anything of this nature. Our aim was to provide a resource which could be picked up for a few minutes and then rejected when the information had been obtained.

Our home-made booklet has every primitive procedure in Logo (RML Logo) explained in it. The explanations are short and to the point. An example of the use of a primitive is given only when its sense cannot be conveyed in any other way. The handbook is intended to be used as a reference, either to remind a child of the syntax of a particular word or when a new word looks as though it might be appropriate for a particular task in hand.

As a consequence of this, the presentation of the booklet is very dry and the children are never involved with it as they would be if it were more contextual. It is not easy to use and children need to be taught to refer to it. For this reason we decided not to use the handbooks for the first few weeks. In the early stages the children really only need a few commands, and we provided the format for the use of FD, BK etc. by designing a large poster. We kept the booklets in a cupboard, and we introduced them very slowly, whenever it seemed appropriate for particular children.

Despite all this caution there was a significant period of time when children tried to use the booklet as a source of ideas. They found a new word, played with it for a while, and then went back to look for another. Thankfully this was a passing phase which did not last too long, and so we could teach the children to refer to it themselves in a sensible way. Perhaps we ought to stress that our children had plenty of time to learn these sorts of skills. Had we been under more pressure we might have decided not to use a handbook at all.

We mentioned a wall poster earlier, which we used to illustrate FD, BK and other essential early commands. We also made use of the classroom walls to display the children's work regularly. This included screendumps together with the computer code, and so the children were encouraged in yet another way to develop projects. We often suggested that the children might like to look at each other's screens occasionally, but the wall display was there for children from other classes too. There was always the danger of copying, but the length of the code was usually prohibitive. Instead, when children examined what others had produced, they often found the seeds of a new idea.

The classroom walls were also used to pin up multiple copies of the many worksheets that we had written. These sheets served several different purposes, and some of them were more useful than others. Possibly the most valuable were the sheets which contained only a single procedure and which were designed to introduce a new concept or technique. The procedure shown in Fig. 4.1 illustrates how to get Logo to ask a question and then to store whatever is typed at the keyboard. The sheet did not have any exercises for the children to tackle, and on its own it did not provide any stimulation. The sheet was useful only when the children had already decided that they wanted this particular technique and that they needed some help to put it into action. Children who are engaged in a project will use a resource like this one in a balanced and sensible way. Once they are committed to the work they are doing, they will readily leave it for a while in order to explore the new idea. Many children typed SPEECH at their own keyboards, and

then they spent some time modifying it slightly, until they were reasonably happy that they could incorporate the new idea into their projects.

Three further examples of similar sheets are shown in Figs. 4.2–4.4. Children often write procedures with a series of commands such as SQ 1, SQ 2, SQ 3 etc., and the sheet in Fig. 4.2 shows them how to deal with this more effectively. The

```
                    Growing Squares

TO SQUARES "SIZE
   IF :SIZE = 200 [STOP]
   SQUARE :SIZE
   SQUARES :SIZE + 20
END

TO SQUARE "SIDE
   REPEAT 4 [FD :SIDE RT 90]
END
```

FIGURE 4.2   Example of a worksheet used to illustrate tail recursion

```
                    Single Key Press

TO DOODLE
   IF KEY? [TURN] [FD 1]
   DOODLE
END

TO TURN
   MAKE "KEY RC
   IF :KEY = "R [RT 20]
   IF :KEY = "L [LT 20]
END
```

FIGURE 4.3   Example of a worksheet used to illustrate single-key input

```
                    Asking Questions

TO SPEECH
   PRINT [WHAT IS YOUR NAME?]
   MAKE "REPLY RL
   PRINT [ ]
   PRINT FPUT "HELLO :REPLY
END
```

FIGURE 4.1   Example of a worksheet used to introduce the idea of user input

sheet in Fig. 4.3 gives two procedures which a few children were able to develop by themselves but which enabled many more to work on projects in which it was necessary to change something by pressing a single key. The final example (Fig. 4.4) is also more advanced, and it shows how recursion works. Many children learned about tail-recursion, where the last line of the procedure calls the procedure again. Full recursion is much more difficult to understand, but one or two children were up to it, and it was important to have the resources available to deal with their needs.

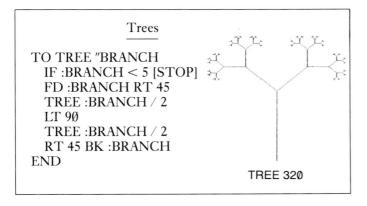

```
                     Trees

TO TREE "BRANCH
    IF :BRANCH < 5 [STOP]
    FD :BRANCH RT 45
    TREE :BRANCH / 2
    LT 90
    TREE :BRANCH / 2
    RT 45 BK :BRANCH
END
                                    TREE 320
```

FIGURE 4.4   Example of a worksheet used to illustrate full recursion

Before we started to teach Logo we prepared a number of sheets which were intended as starters for projects, but these proved to have a very limited use in the classroom. One sheet suggested that a group of children work together to produce anagrams. Each child had to write procedures to draw some different letters, and then the children were asked to combine them to make words. Two other sheets instructed the children to write a quiz and to create a design made from squares. The ideas which were presented were open enough to enable most children to achieve some results, but the children did not seem to become committed to the ideas as they did when the projects grew naturally.

Some other sheets which were available in our classrooms contained challenges of various sorts. We have discussed elsewhere how we wanted to encourage the children to achieve specific objectives sometimes. In general they were free to amend their goals when it suited them, but we also wanted to provide situations where the children were forced to produce a clearly defined pattern. For example, one sheet contained a picture of a chessboard to reproduce on the screen, and another showed a particular configuration of circles.

Some challenges, such as the one which asked the children to find the dimensions of the screen, were appropriate quite early on: 'What is the longest distance the turtle can walk, without falling off the edge?' Others were much harder, giving a program consisting of five or six procedures, together with a drawing of what it was meant to produce, and asking the children to find the two bugs. Since the level of difficulty was so varied we had to be very careful about the way we used the sheets. Any sort of organisation or formal system would have been counter to the aims of our general approach, and so the sheets were available on a voluntary basis. We often directed a child to a particular sheet, but we did not force the issue.

This strategy meant that the children had to learn to make effective decisions about their own work. They had to decide whether or not they needed a sheet and, if they were looking for a challenge, they had to pick an appropriate one. Not all the children learned these skills, but they were not impeded as a

result, and neither were they frustrated by being forced to do something too easy or too difficult.

Away from the computer

It is often helpful for the children to do some work on Logo away from the computers. There may be a long gap between one computer session and the next, especially if there are just one or two machines available. This means that a short period of planning or reviewing would help to maintain the children's enthusiasm. Also, there are some ideas which can be demonstrated to the whole class, and there are games and other activities which might help several children to learn new skills and techniques.

We have already explained how children can learn new ideas from each other by looking at the wall display or listening to their classmates describing new projects. Sometimes we found that it was necessary to introduce a new idea ourselves, because none of the children stumbled across it or asked a question which allowed us to introduce it to them within the context of their work. For example, we had been teaching a group of more able 13–year-old children for three weeks, and none of them had used variables. We did not want to have a formal class lesson, in which all the children were forced to listen to us before they worked through some boring exercises, but we did think it was worthwhile bringing the idea to their attention. Our resolution was to spend ten minutes, away from the computers, explaining to the class how to write a procedure with inputs. We did not dwell on the technicalities at this stage, but we stressed how an input made a procedure more flexible than it was before. In other words, we gave them the idea of inputs so that they could use it later when it was appropriate.

Planning is another Logo activity which needs to be encouraged away from the machines. A professional programmer probably spends more time with pencil and paper than she does at the keyboard. Children need to be encouraged to plan their work, but there are dangers in overemphasising this. The children are learning to program and so they will need to make mistakes, and it is much easier to explore different possibilities at the computer keyboard. When children learn new techniques they need to practise them before they can use them efficiently, and this is not possible without the computer. We have seen some children spend a long time planning a drawing in their exercise books, only to reject the plans altogether when things went wrong.

However, it is useful for the children to do a quick sketch before they start to type. The teacher should make it clear that the children do not have to be bound by every line of their sketch but that it makes working together much easier. It is not that uncommon to see two children having a debate because they are working from different mental images of what it is they want to draw. The sketch will help to focus their activities. Planning will also help to maintain the children's interest between sessions at the machine. Most important of all, when a teacher encourages some planning, she is telling the children to set goals for themselves, and this helps them to develop their own work.

Children can also benefit from reviewing their work occasionally. Open Day always provides a good opportunity for them to write an account of one of their projects. The final presentation might include screendumps, and even a little code, but the main emphasis should be to describe what their program does and how it works.

Interaction

In a Logo classroom there is the potential for a natural, human relationship to develop between teacher and children as they collaborate to solve a problem which arises in one of the children's projects. The role of the teacher becomes more like that of a tutor, and her authority is based on her knowledge and her ability to help, rather than on any extrinsic discipline. When the teacher is seen as cooperating in children's activities, rather than judging them, the relationship between children and teacher can begin to approach the ideal vividly described by Jerome Bruner in *Toward a Theory of Instruction*:

> 'I would like to suggest that what the teacher must be, to be an effective competence model, is a day-to-day working model with whom to interact. It is not so much that the teacher provides a model to *imitate*. Rather, it is that the teacher can become part of the student's internal dialogue — somebody whose respect he wants, someone whose standards he wishes to make his own.'

One factor which contributes to this more natural relationship is that the teacher is often talking to children individually, or in small groups, rather than to the class as a whole. This obviously requires a different manner and tone of voice, and it is made easier if the teacher can sit with the children, rather than standing over them. Of course this may lead to problems if the teacher's attention is completely taken up with one group, to the exclusion of the rest of the class. Simple strategies such as the teacher sitting so that she does not have her back to the rest of the class when talking to a group can help to maintain contact with all the children.

Answering questions

When children are working on their own projects, they want to solve the problems which arise so that they can proceed. They will solve many of them by themselves, as they discuss them with their partners, but sometimes they will demand the teacher's help. A teacher who is unfamiliar with working with Logo may feel unsure about the best way to respond to these requests, since there is a tension between wanting to help the children to get on and wanting them to think out solutions for themselves. The most appropriate strategy in any particular case will naturally depend on the circumstances and in the following examples of some typical questions we have tried to illustrate this.

'How do we move the turtle without drawing any lines?'

Questions like this are quite straightforward. The children know exactly what it is that they want to know. The knowledge that they require is not linked to any conceptual understanding: there is no way that they could work it out for themselves. There is a Logo command to lift the turtle's pen, and the teacher's response must be to provide this information or to direct the children to where they can find it out.

'How do we draw a circle?'

This situation is less simple, and there are several possible levels of response. Because the Logo philosophy emphasises learning rather than teaching, the most obvious response is to regard this as something that children can work out for themselves and to encourage them to do this. Pretending to be the turtle would help the children to understand the need for short forward movements, alternating with small turns. This involves either implicitly or explicitly refusing to answer the children's question directly, and how a teacher does this will depend on the children involved, and the teacher's own style.

Deflecting questions which children could answer for themselves can have positive effects in terms of encouraging independent thinking, but it can also be disconcerting for the children. To them, asking how to draw a circle may not seem any different from asking how to raise the pen, and the teacher's behaviour in answering one question but not the other may seem inconsistent and obstructive. A typical response from children who want a circle in their drawing, and get a lot of talk about walking like the turtle when they ask for help, is 'we'll make the wheels a different shape then'.

If the children asking the question are not fully committed to their project, the teacher may decide that stopping to explore how to draw circles is inappropriate. If the children are working at top-level and have not saved their work as a program, experimenting with the effects of different commands would ruin their picture. The best thing to do here may be to give the children instructions to draw a suitable circle and to spend time later discussing with them how it works.

'How does REPEAT work?'

Here the children probably know the purpose of REPEAT, but they need to be reminded of its syntactic form. Again, the most appropriate response to this sort of question depends very much on the circumstances in which it is posed. A straightforward answer may suffice, but most children will not need very much encouragement to explore commands of the form REPEAT 100 [FD 100 RT 155]. An activity of this nature will provide plenty of practice with the command and allow the children to discover a number of mathematical relationships at the same time.

'How do we get the computer to ask us for instructions?'

The children want to write an interactive program, and they need a new technique. If they are fully committed to the work they are doing, the teacher can suggest that they put their long-term goals aside for a while in order to explore the new idea. The teacher might provide the children with a simple procedure which utilises the technique but does not do exactly what the children want for their project. This would allow a guided discovery approach as the children find out what the new procedure does and how it works. When the children can control the situation well enough, they can incorporate it into their own work.

There are countless questions like these which children ask when their work is important to them. The teacher's response may be to give them information, or she may create a situation where the children can discover the solution for themselves. Although it is not always critical which approach she adopts, it is important that the children feel able to ask the questions in the first place.

Intervention

A common misapprehension has grown up that, in order to encourage children to work independently in Logo, the teacher should not intervene at all. It should be clear by now that we do not agree with this view but see the teacher's input as a vital aspect of the children's learning. However, the non-intervention view does indicate a genuine concern that many teachers try to take far too dominant a role in the children's work, and that their intervention can often inhibit the children from developing their own understanding. In general, our advice would always be for a teacher to stop and think before intervening, giving the children time to think out their own solutions and giving herself time to consider what she is going to say before jumping in. It is important to spend time just watching and listening when children are working at the keyboard, to find out exactly what they are doing, before deciding whether an intervention is necessary or appropriate. It is often tempting to try to introduce a new command or technique before the children are ready for it or to correct an error rather than suggesting how the children could solve the problem for themselves. It is impossible to give hard and fast rules, but never touching the keyboard is a good starting point.

The following story illustrates a typical point at which intervention seems appropriate. Two children are drawing a square.

'It's easy — all you do is FD 5Ø and then RT 9Ø and then FD 5Ø and so on.'

'OK — you type it in, and I'll write it down for later.'

The children are involved in their task, and have drawn part of their square. Their teacher sees a chance to introduce a new technique.

'There's a much quicker way to do that. If you like I'll show you how the REPEAT command works.'

But the children do not seem to appreciate this offer.

'Oh come on Miss, we've only got to do one more line and we've finished.'

This seemed an ideal point for the teacher's intervention; the children were committed to their project, and they clearly understood the work they were doing. The new command was suggested in a friendly, unforced way, and yet the intervention appears to have been unsuccessful. But all was not lost: two weeks later the children wanted to colour in their square, and they realised that it would take them a long time to type in all the commands they needed. They went back to their teacher and asked how to use REPEAT.

Although the intervention seemed to be unsuccessful at first, without it the children would not have asked for the new technique later on. There is a very important distinction for the teacher between giving information and telling children what to do. Had the teacher imposed the new technique by forcing them to use REPEAT straight away, the consequences may not have been so positive. But this did not happen. The teacher made it clear to the children that there was a new command available to them, but she phrased her intervention in such a way that the children were free to reject it.

In fact children working on their own projects in Logo often reject suggestions when they are made, only to come back to them some time later. Children learn new ideas when they are ready for them, and in a crowded classroom it is hardly possible for the teacher to ascertain the needs of each child at exactly the right time. If the teacher's interventions are based on the children's own work, but without any pressure for ideas to be taken up immediately, then children can make the ideas their own when they are ready to.

Asking questions

It is often easier to make interventions in a relaxed way by asking questions. When children are involved with their own projects it is clear that they are the ones who know about the situation and that the teacher is on unfamiliar ground. This is the reverse of the normal situation and can lead to a noticeable change in the kind of dialogue which goes on. In most classrooms, the purpose of almost all the teacher's questions is not to get information but to test what the pupils know. Questioning becomes ritualised by both teacher and pupils and loses its potential as a teaching technique, or even as a normal means of human interaction. In Logo lessons, this questioning ritual can break down, as the teacher is often genuinely asking for information, and the children realise this. (How did you draw that bit? Which procedure draws the eyes? How will you get the turtle back to the right place?) This enables the children to talk more freely: it is a conversation not an interrogation. The children are also free to ignore questions if they do not fully understand them or simply do not like them. This is a very healthy situation, since they are beginning to take control of their own work. Asking appropriate questions can be a powerful way in which the teacher can encourage children to explore extensions to their projects, and introduce new challenges.

Holding back

Holding back from intervening and allowing children time to solve their own problems, to develop their own projects and to control their own pace of work is often an important part of the teacher's role. Time is essential for project work to develop in a natural way.

It takes time for children to become committed to the work they are doing. At the start of a new project, children may work at a relatively low level before they are ready to tackle the more difficult ideas ahead. Teachers often feel that they want to intervene with help and ideas at this stage but, as illustrated in the previous section, their efforts may seem unwelcome.

Children working on Logo projects are able to learn in a natural way because they have control over what they work on, and also because they can control *when* they tackle difficult ideas. Often, children who have tackled new and difficult ideas in one lesson then go back to activities they have done before or change to much simpler activities. For example Rupa and Kim were trying to make a tessellating pattern with hexagons. Their teacher encouraged them to look for a larger unit that they could repeat, and they struggled with the problems involved in drawing this ring of hexagons (Fig. 4.5). In the next lesson, they tried to tessellate this new shape, but it proved very difficult. So they saw the shape as a football, and spent the rest of the lesson drawing a boot with a simple, unstructured linear procedure (Fig 4.6). At first glance, this may seem a negative aspect of allowing children to work on their own projects, since it looks as though the girls simply gave up. In fact, if they had not felt free to alter their goal and to tackle something well within their abilities, they may have continued to struggle with the tessellation problem and become very disheartened. By changing their goal, they were able to produce a drawing that they were pleased with, and they were confident about moving on to the challenge of a new project in future lessons.

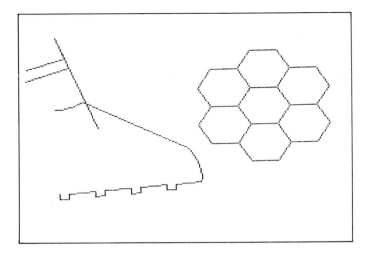

FIGURE 4.6   A picture that resulted when it proved to be too difficult to tessellate with the ring of hexagons

Alan showed a similar need to alter the rate at which he tackled difficult ideas when he asked whether he could work alone for a few lessons. Alan had problems with much of his school work, particularly in language and mathematics. He had been working for most of the year with Rashid, a much brighter boy. They had worked well together at first, but gradually it was clear that Alan was contributing less and less to the partnership. On his own, Alan soon settled down to a project which was much simpler than the one he had been working on with Rashid but which involved what were, for him, some difficult ideas about angle and calculating distances. He needed a lot of help and support from his teacher at first, but he clearly found the work rewarding. After a few weeks, Alan went back to working with Rashid and joined in the discussions about the project with much more confidence, even though many of the ideas that Rashid was now using were much more difficult than those Alan had tackled on his own.

Superficially, it may seem that children like Alan, Rupa and Kim, and children who are just starting work on their projects, are wasting time by working at a low level. It can be hard for a teacher to resist the temptation to try to put pressure on such children to get on with something worthwhile. The long-term benefits of holding back at this point can be considerable, but it takes confidence.

Encouraging projects

In most of their lessons in school, children are used to having the teacher make decisions about the work they are going to do, so they are not used to taking control of their own learning. If a teacher wants children to work in a more independent way and to develop their own projects, she must teach them how to do this. One step towards this is to give explicit instructions about carrying work over from one lesson to the next, which might

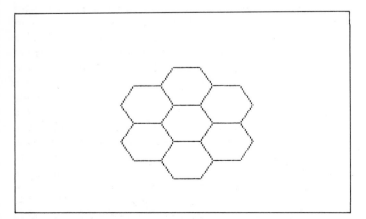

FIGURE 4.5   Example of an attempt to tessellate with hexagons

include how to save files on disc, or making provision for safe storage of floor turtle drawings. She can also stress that she wants the children to set their own goals and give public praise to those children who start on projects. Another useful approach is to organise regular short sessions in which children who have started to develop projects talk to the rest of the class about what they have been doing and what they intend to do next. Such sessions also give an opportunity to introduce powerful ideas, like using the editor, to the whole class. Not all the children may be ready to use these ideas themselves, and they certainly will not learn *how* to use them in these sessions, but they will have the chance to see possibilities that they may want to use in the future.

Setting appropriate challenges

Most of this book has emphasised the value of children developing their own projects, and making decisions about what they want to work on, but it is often appropriate for teachers to set challenges for children to work on. These challenges may arise out of a problem that children encounter. For example, the teacher may suggest that children explore a particular technique or command that they need to use in their project, by setting a challenge which makes the use of the command easy to understand. If children are trying to draw regular polygons, the value of using REPEAT may not be obvious, since each line looks different because of its orientation. A group of 14-year-olds who were fairly new to Logo had this problem, and their teacher set them a challenge with the floor turtle. They had designed a race-track, and the challenge was to instruct the turtle to complete five laps. The effect of REPEAT was obvious to the children in this situation.

At other times it may be appropriate for the teacher to set children challenges that are not connected with projects. This may be when children have completed a project and are at rather a loose end, or when children are having difficulty in settling down to directing their own work. There are always some children who take a long time to get involved in a particular project. A challenge suggested by the teacher can engage their interest and may even provide the starting point for a project of their own, provided that the children are not constrained by the task but realise that they are free to extend or adapt, or even to ignore, it. Challenges may be suggested directly by the teacher or indirectly by means of posters and other stimulus material. Since there is never one 'right' way to solve a problem in Logo, it is possible for children with differing abilities and experience to work on the same problem, and this can provide useful opportunities for learning from each other. We described a situation of this kind in Chapter 1, when three pairs at Bridgeton had been given the pattern of squares to work on.

A similar situation occurred in one of our lessons. At the end of the lesson two screens showed almost identical patterns of overlapping octagons, inspired by one of the posters around the room. Although the results on the screen were similar, the programs the girls had written were quite different. Hazel and Leena had written four short procedures, which drew an octagon, moved the turtle to the correct starting position and repeated the octagon and a forward move 14 times. In contrast, Linda had written a much longer program, which called six separate procedures to draw the six octagons in her pattern. Each of these procedures began by sending the turtle HOME and then moving it to the correct starting position and drawing an octagon. The six procedures were identical, except for the distance that the turtle moved before drawing each octagon.

Hazel and Leena's program was clearly more elegant and economical, showing a much greater understanding of the power of modular programming: it is the kind of program an experienced adult programmer might write. Linda's program contained many features which indicate that she does not yet understand the power of using sub-procedures, but nevertheless her program achieved the effect she wanted on the screen, and she was justifiably pleased with it. Although Linda was working at quite a different level from Hazel and Leena, it was quite possible for the girls to work alongside each other in the same group without many of the normal problems of mixed ability teaching. It was also possible for them to look at, and talk about, each other's work, and to learn from each other.

Another reason why a teacher might decide to set a particular challenge for a child or a group of children is when she wants to focus their attention on a particular bit of mathematics that can be fruitfully explored in Logo. We will discuss several examples of this kind in Chapters 5 and 6.

Errors

Another way in which the children can take control of their own work in Logo is in judging their own success or failure. Because they have set their own goals, and have instant feed-back from the computer, the children do not need the teacher to say whether their work is 'right' or 'wrong'. In fact, we are often put in our places if we say 'That's nice' in response to an attractive display on the screen by being told, 'No, it isn't what we wanted at all!' Children who are used to having all their work 'marked' by a teacher may take some time to get over seeing errors as wrong and something to be ashamed of, and they will need encouragement from their teacher to change this view. Promoting de-bugging as a respectable and enjoyable activity is one way of developing a positive attitude to errors, and even using the term 'bugs' instead of 'mistakes' helps to overcome existing prejudices.

An important feature of Logo is the error messages which appear on the screen if a command is typed which the computer cannot interpret. In LCSI Logo the messages are relatively clear and friendly. However, children and many adults seem not to read these messages at first or find them difficult to interpret. In the early stages of programming, most error messages will in fact reflect typing errors, e.g. I DON'T KNOW HOW TO FD100, I DON'T KNOW HOW TO EDIT"FRED. Since what was actually typed will still be on the screen, this provides a good opportunity for children to learn to read error messages, even though they may realise what their mistake was straight away. In more complex programs, error messages can give more detailed information. In one of our classes a group of girls had written a procedure C which called another procedure P, which they had not yet written. When they ran C they got the unforgettable message I DON'T KNOW HOW TO P IN C.

Learning to read and use error messages is an important step for children in learning to program and in taking responsibility for their own work. As the children's programs become more sophisticated, de-bugging becomes a more important, and more difficult, activity. This is often best done away from the computer, as we describe in Chapter 7 on structured programming.

Knowing how and when it is best to intervene when children are working in Logo is by no means easy or straightforward, and it is not always obvious what the effect of our actions has been. If we want to avoid imposing ourselves upon children and dominating their thinking, then we have to find ways of working which encourage children to take the initiative for the activities with which they engage and for the acquisition of knowledge. We have to put the children firmly in control of their own learning. We can do this by allowing children to develop their own projects and to create their own goals. Then our interventions can be based on their work and, even if we jump in with both feet, the children will be able to make use of our help as and when they need it.

5 Mathematical Content

The discipline of mathematics can be divided into the two aspects of content and process. When children learn mathematics, they need to know the content of the various topics which have become part of our heritage, and at the same time they must learn to solve problems and to think mathematically. This division is actually rather artificial, since mathematical thinking must apply most readily to mathematical content, and children should practise both aspects whenever they learn mathematics. The study of investigation should not really be seen as something separate, but it is not yet a common feature of most classrooms, and while it is new it does no harm to consider it as something special. In this chapter we will describe the mathematical content which arises when children learn Logo, and we will discuss the thinking processes in Chapter 6.

Angle

Turtle geometry is obviously very rich in mathematics. It was designed specifically to produce an environment for the study of geometry, and one concept which pervades everything the children do is angle. Angle is probably the most difficult of the measures that children meet in school, since it is not immediately obvious what it is that is being measured. Many children who have had 'traditional' lessons about angle, and even the use of protractors, would be unsure which of the two angles in Fig. 5.1 is the larger.

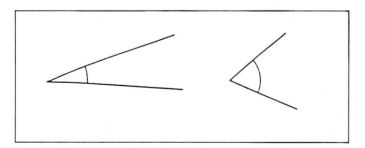

FIGURE 5.1   Difficulties with angle measurement

This confusion arises because of the need to appreciate the dynamic nature of a turn, as well as the static concept of the two lines drawn on a page. It is difficult to get across the dynamic aspect of angle in print, so it is hardly surprising that textual resources concentrate on drawings. Children need to experience angle in terms of turning by means of physical activities; opening doors, turning on taps, using scissors, moving the hand of a toy clock and, perhaps most important, their own body movements. Most primary school teachers build this kind of experience into the early stages of children's learning about angle, and this is often linked to learning about left and right or compass directions. The difficulty comes when more formal comparison and measurement of angles are required. Physical movements do not normally leave a trace that can be measured, and it is difficult to link them directly and accurately to units of measurement, and so the focus inevitably moves to static drawings and measuring instruments.

The turtle, and particularly the floor turtle, can provide an intermediate experience between physical movements and formal measurement of angles. When many people, both children and adults, first meet a turtle they expect the commands RT and LT to make the turtle *move* to the left or the right and are surprised when it remains in one position. In the case of the screen turtle, it may not even be obvious that the turtle has rotated, since it is instantly re-drawn in its new orientation. Some teachers use 'slow turtle' procedures for young children to make the turning of the screen turtle clearer. These simply use REPEAT to turn the turtle 1° a number of times:

```
TO R "N                 TO L "N
  REPEAT :N [RT 1]         REPEAT :N [LT 1]
END                     END
```

The final effect of R 3Ø is the same as RT 3Ø; the turtle turns right through 30°. The difference is that you can see the turtle turning, since it is re-drawn on the screen each time it turns through 1°.

With a floor turtle, the rotation is slow and clear, and the children can stand behind the turtle and make a direct link between the turtle's movements and their own. This is one respect in which a turtle's movements are different from those of a person or a real animal, which can turn and move forward *at the same time*. Working with a floor turtle (or a programmable toy like Bigtrak or George) makes the distinction between the two kinds of movement (travelling a distance and rotating) very clear. When a turtle rotates, nothing is drawn; only the orientation of the turtle is changed. The fact that

Logo requires an imput (a number) with the commands RT and LT makes it clear that the size of the turtle's turn can be measured.

Teachers of young children are often concerned that their pupils will be unable to control the turtle's turns because they do not know how to measure angles in degrees. Perhaps because of this worry, Bigtrak's turns are related to minutes on a clock-face; the instruction to turn left through a right angle is ← 15. In practice, children do not seem to be bothered either by using degrees with the turtle or by transfering from 'Bigtrak turns' to 'turtle turns'. They seem to see the numbers relating to turns as they see those relating to forward movement; they are numbers that the turtle under-stands, and the children become familiar with them by trial and error. Only later will the children learn that, although 'turtle steps' are not fixed units, the numbers relating to turtle turns work in exactly the same way for all turtles. They will find that particular numbers, such as 90 and 360, are important. Later, this knowledge can be linked to other work on the measurement of angles, and it may lead to more sophisticated investigations into angle properties. One exam-ple of this was Afzal's project which is described later in this chapter.

However, although children who have worked with turtles will have a strong dynamic concept of angle, the transfer to understanding static angle may not be a smooth one. When a turtle moves and turns and moves again, the trace that it leaves does not show the angle that it has turned through (Fig 5.2). Children (and adults) who have met the formal

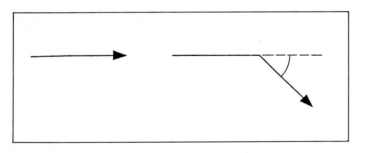

FIGURE 5.2   An angle produced by a turtle

representation of angles before they work with a turtle often type REPEAT 3 [FD 100 RT 60] with the intention of drawing a triangle, because their attention is on the internal angles, rather than the turtle's path. Children who have grown up with turtles may have a parallel problem when faced with comparing the sizes of static angles. They will need to be told to imagine that the turtle is stationary, at the 'point' of the angle, facing along one of the lines, and then turning to face along the other one. This is not a situation that often occurs spontaneously when children are working on their own projects, so it may be appropriate to set up situations to allow children to experience this (perhaps by playing turtle or using

the floor turtle) when they need to transfer their dynamic understanding of angles to static situations.

Number

Numbers are an important part of the Logo learning environment, and children working with turtles will naturally be involved with using numbers continually. Logo can contribute to the young child's developing understanding of number in several ways. The most obvious is in the calculations of both lengths and angles which inevitably arise when children are drawing. Children rarely seem to need to use pencil and paper for these: getting the picture right is a strong motivation for accurate mental arithmetic.

For young children particularly, Logo provides an unusual opportunity to get a feel for large numbers. An understanding of small numbers can be developed through experience of sets of objects, but it is much more difficult to understand larger numbers in the same way. You can count and see and handle seven objects, but this is not so easy with 17 or 97. Because turtle steps and degrees are very small, children have to use comparatively large numbers as soon as they begin working with the turtle. As they draw with the turtle, they experiment with large numbers and get a feeling for their relative sizes by linking them to the lengths of lines or the sizes of angles. There are very few other activities which can offer young children this kind of opportunity to *use* large numbers in a meaningful way rather than simply manipulating symbols on paper.

Working at the keyboard, children are, of course, often just manipulating symbols. A young child may press the key labelled '4' two or three times to get an imput for FD without any understanding of place value and the relationship between 4, 44 and 444. She may not even know how to say the larger numbers, but she will get some idea of the effect of repeating digits by seeing the relative sizes of the lines that are drawn. Almost all children enjoy testing the turtle by trying to find the largest number that they can put after FD or BK. This is a valuable experience, which will enrich more formal learning about place value.

Since primitives like FD and RT will accept decimal fractions and negative numbers, as well as positive whole numbers, as inputs, older children may also gain an intuitive feel for different kinds of numbers through their work in Logo. Later in this chapter there is some discussion of the use of Logo to introduce directed numbers.

Estimation

Closely linked with the idea of getting a feel for large numbers is the skill of estimation. Most primary mathematics schemes give a lot of attention to developing estimation skills in relation to standard units of measure, but in general the activities which they suggest have little meaning for the children. Typically children are asked to estimate, say, the length of various objects in the classroom to the nearest suitable unit and then to check their estimate by measuring. This may be an effective way of practising estimation, but it is otherwise a pretty pointless activity: in any real case you would not need to estimate if you have a measuring instrument available. Since most children are anxious to get their answers 'right', they often measure first and then invent a close estimate.

When children are drawing with a turtle, they are forced to make frequent estimates of the lengths they want to draw, since FD requires an input. The turtle gives instant feed-back on how accurate their estimate was and encourages more sophisticated estimation skills, progressively homing in on a target. This is perhaps most effective with a floor turtle, where the distances travelled are greater, the turtle moves slowly and it is not easy to rub out if you overshoot. For young children who are working with a screen turtle, some teachers find it helpful to write procedures to make the turtle move more slowly. This can be done by replacing, say, FD 100 with REPEAT 100 [FD 1], in the same way as the procedures for slow turns. An additional advantage of the floor turtle is that its pen leaves a blob each time the turtle stops, and so provides a record of the successive estimates.

Estimating when you are drawing with a turtle is quite different from the apparently pointless activities used to practise estimation in metres or grams. The estimation has a real purpose, and so there is a powerful motivation to become more accurate in your estimates. Developing this confidence with estimation is a valuable skill even though turtle steps do not relate to any of the standard units of measurement. In most real life situations, being able to make a reasonable estimate is not a matter of giving an absolute value in standard units but of estimating in relation to the information you already have. This may be done in a variety of ways; by comparison by eye with other known lengths, by using an informal measuring instrument (such as your hand), by doing an approximate calculation based on any measurements you already know, or a combination of these. These are exactly the ways in which children do estimate lengths in Logo.

Inverses

When children are working in direct drive, they often make mistakes in the way that they move or turn the turtle, and they want to undo their commands. With a floor turtle, lines cannot be rubbed out, and so errors may often be incorporated into a new drawing. On the screen, a line can be rubbed out by typing PE (pen erase) and then moving exactly over the line. The easiest way to do this is to go backwards, without changing the heading of the turtle, but this is not immediately obvious to young children. Working with the turtle gives them the opportunity, and a reason, to experiment with undoing commands and to get an intuitive idea of inverse operations: BK 100 undoes FD 100 etc.

A common error in turning the turtle is to go left instead of right, and young children may also find it difficult to know how to correct this. Their first attempts will almost certainly be to return the turtle to its original heading, before making the correct turn. It is quite a big step to see that, if you type RT 30 instead of LT 30, this can be corrected just by typing LT 60.

Inverse operations in mathematics are very difficult for children to grasp; hence the fascination of 'think of a number' puzzles. Although turtle commands are not directly linked to arithmetic operations, the idea of doing and undoing is an important starting point that could be drawn on in later, more formal, work.

Formal recording

When young children are learning mathematics, there is always a difficulty in moving on from the practical activities and discussion, which are essential for developing concepts, to formal, symbolic recording. There are really two problems. The first is that mathematical symbols are very abstract and very condensed. It is difficult to make the links between the symbols and what they stand for, and all too often children are encouraged to learn rules for manipulating the symbols without understanding what the symbols mean. The second problem is that although formal recording has a purpose for the teacher, this is not immediately clear to the children. From the children's point of view, the only purpose for the recording may be to allow the teacher to mark their work: it has no direct value for the children's own mathematics. Consider, for instance, a child who writes $5 \div 25$ when she means $25 \div 5$. We often say 'fives into 25' and we write $5\overline{)25}$, but $5 \div 25$ means something different. The child may understand division, but the formal language is either confusing or leaves the child cold. After all, despite what the teacher might say, the child knows that the teacher really knows just what the child means.

Investigative work may overcome the second of these problems, since the need for keeping some sort of record of results is intrinsic to the activity. However, these are often personal, informal records, which are not transferable to other tasks or easily understood by anyone else.

When children are working in Logo they are forced to use precise formal symbols in order to communicate with the turtle. Children working together on a project soon discover the advantage of using Logo code to communicate with each other as well, since it is clear and unambiguous. These children are using a formal symbol system in the same way that mathematicians do. They do this naturally since it has an intrinsic value for their work, rather than being an artificial task imposed by someone else. Although the recording they use is precise and symbolic, the symbols themselves are not arbitrary (as is often the case in mathematics) but are linked to familiar words and actions. Logo code also follows strict rules of syntax, which has parallels in the conventions needed to express mathematics unambiguously and in the grammar of written languages. While explicitly learning to 'talk' to the turtle in Logo code, young children are also implicitly learning the value of formal, precise methods of written communication.

Coordinates

Every full version of Logo has a coordinate grid system underlying the screen. Usually the origin is at the centre, but RML Logo has its origin at the bottom left-hand corner. The numbering of the axes varies from one computer to another. The axes are not visible, but can be used by means of the commands SETX, SETY and SETPOS. Typing SETPOS [100 50] sends the turtle to the point (100, 50) on the screen without altering its heading. SETX 70 moves the turtle horizontally to the point where $x = 70$ and similarly SETY moves it vertically on the screen. These commands only apply to the screen; they will not be understood by the floor turtle.

Coordinate axes are not a natural part of turtle geometry, in which movements are governed locally by the position and heading of the turtle. Identification with the turtle is not helpful as far as the understanding of an abstract coordinate system is concerned. But SETX and SETY are useful commands when the turtle has to be moved to a specific place on the screen. When Daniel was designing his straight race-course, he needed to draw two horizontal lines:

```
TO TRACK
  CS RT 90
  PU SETPOS [−550 50] PD
  FD 1100
  PU SETPOS [−550 0] PD
  FD 1100
END
```

Daniel knew that he would never need to draw his track in any other position on the screen, and so the use of SETPOS was more convenient than FD, BK, RT and LT.

It is interesting that children spontaneously move the turtle in the x and y directions when they want to get it to a particular point on the screen. It seems to be more comfortable to move horizontally or vertically than to turn first and then to move diagonally. Both strategies require two estimates, but children may be happier with estimating lengths only, rather than a length and an angle, and also with estimating lengths that are parallel to the edges of the screen. The result of this is that children working with turtles probably develop an implicit understanding of coordinates and easily accept the use of SETX and SETY. If a teacher wants to introduce coordinates explicitly as part of the mathematics curriculum, it would probably be a good idea to let children explore SETPOS first: 'Can you draw a picture using only SETPOS, and not FD, BK, LT and RT?'

Visualisation

When children write procedures, they are often following the path of the turtle mentally. Mental work with number and the visualisation of shape are not generally given enough attention in mathematics at school level. This is not to imply that we should revive the old 'mental arithmetic' tests, which only really served to train children's memories. It is important, however, that children develop a mental facility with numbers, so that they do not always have to rely on memorising facts. For instance, children should be able to calculate $103 - 96$ or 7×99 without recourse to pencil and paper or a calculator. It is also important to be able to visualise geometrical ideas. For instance, children might be asked to close their eyes and to count how many edges a cube has, or to imagine the shape of the cross-section when a cube is sliced in a non-symmetric way.

Children who have recently learned to write procedures may still do most of their thinking at top-level. It is quite common for one child to type at the keyboard while the other keeps a written record of the commands. When the drawing is to the children's satisfaction, they write a procedure. Later on the children will be likely to use the editor straight away for more routine tasks, and this means that they are writing the code without seeing the turtle move. They are then visualising the path of the turtle.

Linda and Carol had been creating a creature called Pumpfry (Fig. 5.3). The procedures which the girls had written were most elegant. There was a different sub-procedure for each part of the drawing, and the main outline was produced by repeating 120 times one part of the circle together with one of the spikes.

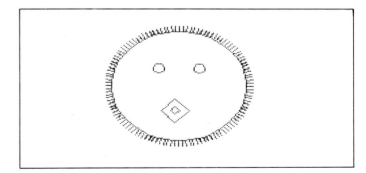

FIGURE 5.3 Pumpfry: a picture produced with sub-procedures

```
TO PUMPFRY1
  REPEAT 120 [PUMPFRY]
END

TO PUMPFRY
  REPEAT 3 [FD 5 RT 1]
  LT 90 FD 15 BK 15 RT 90
END
```

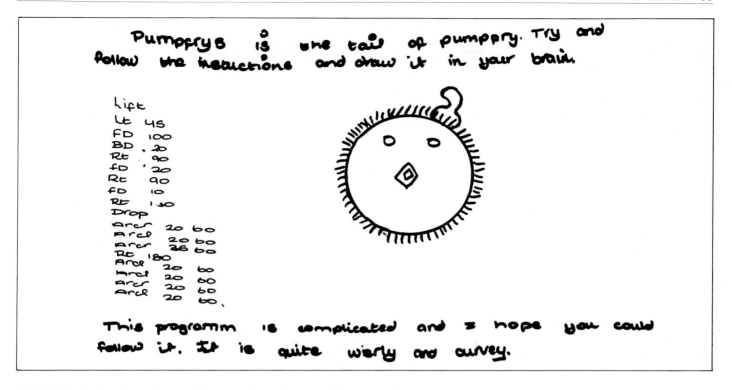

FIGURE 5.4   Linda's write-up of Pumpfry illustrating the skills of visualisation

Later on Linda and Carol added a tail, and when Linda wrote about their work for an Open Day display she made explicit reference to the skills of visualisation (Fig 5.4).

Introducing variables

The use of inputs with Logo procedures provides a real context for the concept of variables. From the start the children learn that the input associated with FD or LT can be any number. Later on, when they design their own procedures to have inputs, they are creating their own variables. One of the easiest entry points to this concept is the variation of the length of a line.

```
TO ARROWHEAD "SIZE
   RT 30 FD :SIZE BK :SIZE
   LT 60 FD :SIZE BK :SIZE
   RT 30
END
```

The procedure ARROWHEAD is similar to FD in the sense that it must always be followed by a number, and this number will provide the value of SIZE (:SIZE) while the procedure is active. Thus ARROWHEAD 20 will draw a small arrow, and ARROWHEAD 50 will be larger. When it is a length which is being varied, the effect of different inputs is fairly obvious.

While children are working on their own projects, they are unlikely to want to vary such a simple shape as an arrowhead. It is more common to find situations where children have drawn a picture, and then they decide that they would like another, smaller version of the same thing. Some time after Carol had finished Pumpfry with Linda, she teamed up with Richard, and Pumpfry reappeared in a different guise. The result was a family of hedgehogs (Fig. 5.5).

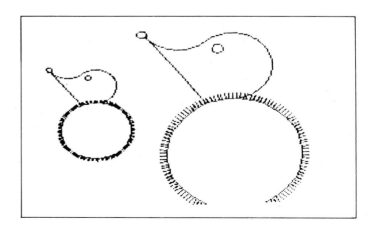

FIGURE 5.5   Hedgehogs of different sizes produced by editing procedures

The program for the original hedgehog was made from four procedures. HOG1 and HOG were renamed versions of PUMPFRY1 and PUMPFRY. HEAD was made from three circular arcs and a straight line, and EYE was a whole circle. Once the hedgehog was completed, Carol and Richard decided that it needed a baby. While writing the new procedures, they realised that they were the same as the old ones in every way except that the lengths were smaller. They also learned that halving each length would preserve the hedgehog shape which they had previously designed. Rather than type out the four procedures again, all the children needed to do to write SMALLHOG1, SMALLHOG, SMALLHEAD and SMALLEYE was to edit the original versions and to change the titles at the same time. The result was FAMILY:

```
TO FAMILY
  HOG1
  HEAD
  EYE
  PU SETPOS [−300 0] PD
  SMALLHOG1
  SMALLHEAD
  SMALLEYE
END
```

Their teacher had hoped that Richard and Carol would continue to refine the procedures by giving them inputs, but the two hedgehogs they had drawn nearly filled the screen. The children had developed an understanding of the concept, and they could see no purpose in being able to draw more hedgehogs of different sizes.

However, Kim and Rupa did want hearts of many different sizes for their Valentine's card (Fig. 5.6). They had started by drawing one heart — the largest:

FIGURE 5.6   Hearts of different sizes produced by using a variable in the procedure

```
TO KISS
  RT 20
  REPEAT 180 [FD 2 RT 1]
  RT 180
  PU REPEAT 180 [FD 2 LT 1] PD
  RT 130
  REPEAT 180 [FD 2 LT 1]
  LT 10 FD 300
  LT 100 FD 340
END
```

In order to draw smaller hearts of different sizes, the girls included a variable which they divided into every length:

```
TO KISS "X
  RT 20
  REPEAT 180 [FD 2 / :X RT 1]
  RT 180
  PU REPEAT 180 [FD 2 / :X LT 1] PD
  RT 130
  REPEAT 180 [FD 2 / :X LT 1]
  LT 10 FD 300 / :X
  LT 100 FD 340 / :X
END
```

Their Valentine's card was then drawn using KISS 1 for the largest heart, and KISS 2, KISS 3 etc. for the others.

Most children started to use variables in the same way as Carol, Richard, Kim and Rupa did. They amended a procedure which drew a picture of a particular size by dividing (or multiplying) all FD and BK commands by a variable quantity. This is in contrast to the standard Logo textbook introduction, in which a variable is used directly to replace certain quantities. The ARROWHEAD procedure at the beginning of this section was written so that :SIZE directly replaced all inputs to FD and BK. This version is much tidier than one like KISS, which a learner might produce:

```
TO ARROWHEAD "SIZE
  RT 30 FD 100 / :SIZE BK 100 / :SIZE
  LT 60 FD 100 / :SIZE BK 100 / :SIZE
  RT 30
END
```

The earlier version of ARROWHEAD is also much easier to use than this one. The purpose of :SIZE is much clearer. But as so often happens when children learn in a natural and unforced way, they do not necessarily leap to the neatest and most efficient solution when they are first presented with a new problem or a new idea.

Shapes and variables

It is not uncommon for children to use REPEAT to draw regular polygons and then to create further designs by repeating the shape. Afzal was in a low fourth-year set at his secondary school, and he had only been learning Logo for a few weeks when he began his project. He had been exploring in what appeared to be a quite random way, when he chanced upon a striking pattern.

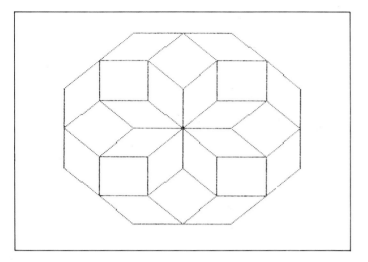

FIGURE 5.7   An example of a pattern produced by using REPEAT

Afzal had not set out to draw the design shown in Fig. 5.7, and part of his delight when it first appeared stemmed from the fact that it is not obvious that it was produced from octagons. Afzal had typed REPEAT 10 [OCT RT 45]. OCT was a procedure which he had written earlier:

```
TO OCT
   REPEAT 8 [FD 100 RT 45]
END
```

The command which produced the lovely pattern was just one of many similar commands, and the fact that he instructed the turtle to draw ten octagons and not eight reveals the exploratory nature of the work.

One of the features of Logo is the ease with which children can switch between exploratory activities and goal-directed work. Without the computer children often seem to get stuck with a particular problem, or they explore without any real purpose, but in Logo explorations often suggest challenges, and challenges lead to further explorations. Afzal's work is a good example of these two complementary sorts of activity. He was excited about his pattern and it clearly had much mathematical potential, and so his teacher suggested that he explore patterns with other shapes and see whether any of them were as appealing as the rotation of octagons. This meant, of course, that he would first need to be goal directed and to write procedures for other regular polygons.

Afzal found the correct angles for the regular polygons by trial and error. He wrote the four procedures in Fig. 5.8 without too many problems. A turning point came when he wanted to find the correct angle for a regular heptagon, which has seven sides. Having used trial and error, he knew that the angle had to be in the region of 51° or 52°. It was described in Chapter 1 how he was dissatisfied with both of these options, and this provided the motivation for him to accept his teacher's advice to tabulate his results systematically as shown in Table 5.1.

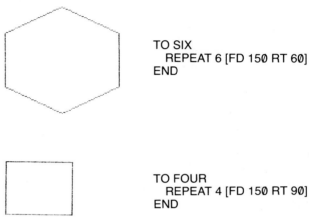

```
TO SIX
   REPEAT 6 [FD 150 RT 60]
END
```

```
TO FOUR
   REPEAT 4 [FD 150 RT 90]
END
```

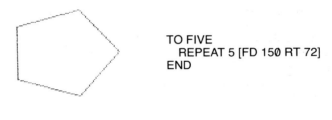

```
TO FIVE
   REPEAT 5 [FD 150 RT 72]
END
```

```
TO THREE
   REPEAT 3 [FD 150 RT 120]
END
```

FIGURE 5.8   Procedures used to draw regular polygons

TABLE 5.1   Afzal's results for regular polygons

Shape	Number of sides	Repeat	Angle
Triangle	3	3	120°
Square	4	4	90°
Pentagon	5	5	72°
Hexagon	6	6	60°
Heptagon	7	7	?
Octagon	8	8	45°

Afzal was then able to spot that the number of sides multiplied by the angle was always 360°. He probably already had some idea of this. Working with a turtle, children do get an intuitive sense of the total turtle trip theorem which says that, whatever the path, if a turtle ends up with the same heading at the end of its trip, the total amount of turn must be 360° or a multiple of 360°. But the table of results made this explicit for Afzal, who was then able to articulate that the angle he wanted for the heptagon would give 360° when it was multiplied by 7.

However, Afzal did not appreciate that he could find the answer by dividing, and his teacher showed him how to work it out on the computer by typing PRINT 360/7. This gave 51.4285715, which he used to draw the shape on the screen before writing the angle in his table. It was then a fairly easy step for him to generalise and write one procedure to draw any regular polygon:

```
TO POLYGON "SIDES
   REPEAT :SIDES [FD 100 RT 360 / :SIDES]
END
```

Having struggled at these goal-directed tasks, Afzal was very happy to spend some time exploring again, and he used his POLYGON procedure to draw the pattern shown in Fig. 5.9.

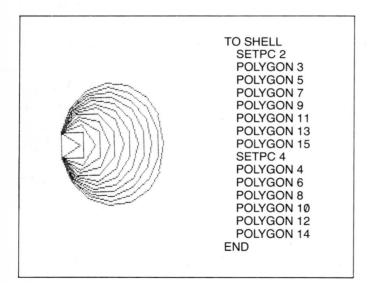

```
TO SHELL
   SETPC 2
   POLYGON 3
   POLYGON 5
   POLYGON 7
   POLYGON 9
   POLYGON 11
   POLYGON 13
   POLYGON 15
   SETPC 4
   POLYGON 4
   POLYGON 6
   POLYGON 8
   POLYGON 10
   POLYGON 12
   POLYGON 14
END
```

FIGURE 5.9 Pattern produced using a generalised procedure for drawing regular polygons 360. Afzal

His final challenge was to draw further patterns like his rotated octagons. He wrote PAT, and it required the same sort of understanding as POLYGON had done before:

```
TO PAT "NUM "SIDES
   REPEAT :NUM [POLYGON :SIDES RT 360 /
   :NUM]
END
```

Afzal was then able to explore many different patterns (Fig. 5.10).

Katrina and Alison had written a similar procedure to POLYGON. Theirs was called SHAPE and it contained an additional variable which allowed the polygons to be drawn in different sizes:

```
TO SHAPE "SIDES "LENGTH
   REPEAT :SIDES [FD :LENGTH LT 360 /
   :SIDES]
END
```

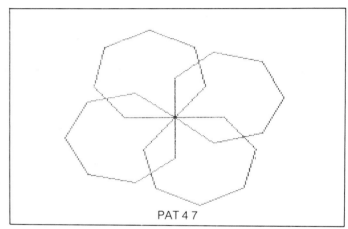

PAT 4 7

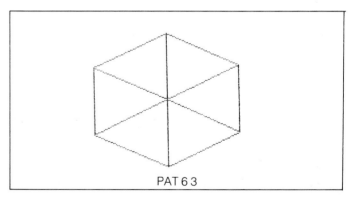

PAT 6 3

FIGURE 5.10 Examples of patterns produced using a procedure to draw any number of regular polygons around a point

Having worked at various activities which involved spirals in their mathematics class, they decided to draw a spiral of decreasing squares (Fig. 5.11). Although their procedure was effective, it was very long, and the use of variables allowed them to produce a similar pattern of triangles much more effectively. First of all they had to write a single procedure (SH2) which would replace each of the lines of TUNNEL. These lines were all the same apart from the colour and the size of the shape, and so they needed two variables.

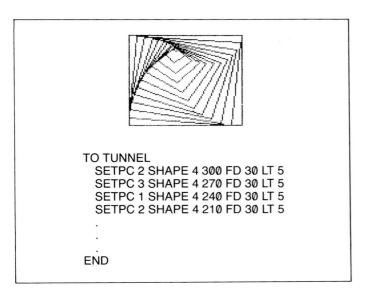

```
TO TUNNEL
    SETPC 2 SHAPE 4 300 FD 30 LT 5
    SETPC 3 SHAPE 4 270 FD 30 LT 5
    SETPC 1 SHAPE 4 240 FD 30 LT 5
    SETPC 2 SHAPE 4 210 FD 30 LT 5
    .
    .
    .
END
```

FIGURE 5.11   Example of a pattern produced using a long procedure without variables

```
TO SH2 "LEN "COL
    SETPC :COL
    SHAPE 3 :LEN
    FD 30
    LT 5
END
```

Katrina and Alison were then able to produce the spiral of triangles shown in Fig. 5.12 with a much shorter procedure.

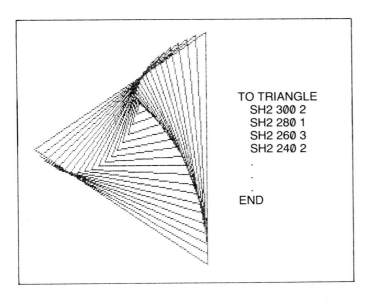

```
TO TRIANGLE
    SH2 300 2
    SH2 280 1
    SH2 260 3
    SH2 240 2
    .
    .
    .
END
```

FIGURE 5.12   Example of a pattern similar to that of Figure 5.11 that was produced using procedures with variables

With a lot of help, the girls made further use of variables to write TRIANGLE as a short recursive procedure, and they consolidated this idea by drawing a pattern of circular spirals in which each arm is made of a number of arcs, with the radius of each arc increasing as it moves away from the centre (Fig. 5.13).

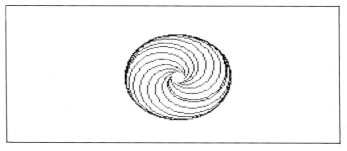

FIGURE 5.13   Example of a pattern produced using variables and recursion

The use of variables to generalise expressions is the essence of algebra, and giving procedures inputs provides a real context in which to use variables. The concept of variable was at the heart of Katrina and Alison's work. When they wrote SH2, they had to be able to pick out the features of TUNNEL which were changing from one line of code to the next and to replace the numbers with a word. Afzal also generalised his individual procedures (SIX, FOUR etc.) in order to write POLYGON, which could then be used to draw any regular polygon.

In Afzal's procedure, the variable called SIDES can take any numerical value, just as x can take any value in the expression

$$(x + 1)^2 = x^2 + 2x + 1$$

Rather than beginning with numerical examples, this identity is often introduced through the manipulation of symbols:

$$(x + 1)^2 = (x + 1)(x + 1)$$
$$= \ldots$$

At the very best some sort of diagram may be produced in support (Fig. 5.14). Numbers are then substituted for x to show that it really does work:

$$(8 + 1)^2 = 8^2 + 2 \times 8 + 1$$

In many traditional algebra courses the ability to manipulate symbols is paramount, and the concept of variable is almost overlooked. Mathematics textbooks offer many opportunities for children to substitute numerical values into algebraic expressions, but in Logo the work with numbers comes first, and when there is a need for more generality the child creates a variable.

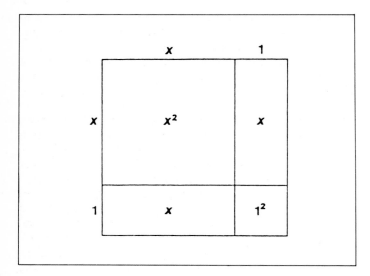

FIGURE 5.14   Example of a diagram used to illustrate algebra: $(x + 1)^2 = x^2 + 2x + 1$

Functions

The concept of function is inherent in Logo. A procedure can be designed so that it has an output, and in this case its behaviour mirrors that of a mathematical function. For instance, the procedure F below is equivalent to the function 'add 2', and G is equivalent to $x \rightarrow 3x$:

```
TO F "NUMBER          TO G "X
  OP :NUMBER + 2          OP :X * 3
END                   END
```

These procedures are operations, and they produce a result. If you type PRINT F 5, the number 7 will be printed on the screen. FD G 20 instructs the turtle to move forwards 60 units. Operations can be combined, so that the output of one procedure becomes the input of another. Thus PRINT F G 10 means that 32 will be printed on the screen, whereas PRINT G F 10 produces 36. Notice how the functions are written in the reverse order when they are combined, in exactly the same way as mathematical functions.

Most of the procedures which children use in turtle geometry are commands rather than operations. FD and RT are used directly and they have an immediate effect. There are, however, many primitive procedures which are operations. XCOR and YCOR each have an output. They produce the x and y coordinates of the turtle's position on the screen. SQRT needs one input, and its output is the square root of the input. RANDOM and OPPS are two further primitive procedures which both have an output and which children are likely to need at one time or another.

The idea of output is very powerful in Logo programming, and while many of the children we taught used operations like SQRT without any difficulty, we never found the right opportunities to teach them about the OP command. The children's projects did not present situations in which OP would have been a valuable asset, and so we have no experience of teaching the idea explicitly. Nevertheless we are confident that the children are now in a far stronger position to be able to understand the concept of function.

Transformation geometry

The mathematical topics which have been discussed in this chapter arise naturally, without explicit teaching, when children use Logo. The same is true of many ideas from transformation geometry. Children get an intuitive grasp of rotation through many of the random patterns which they design. In the earlier section on introducing variables it was described how children create enlargements of their pictures. Reflection too can arise spontaneously. Mandy once asked her teacher about the 'other half' of a picture she was drawing.

'I've done the left-hand part. Is there an easy way to draw the other half?'
'You could use the same procedure Mandy, but you'd need to edit it somehow.'
'I'm not sure how. Could you add 90° to all the angles?'
This was not correct, but her teacher left her to try for herself. Ten minutes later, the teacher returned.
'Well, did you do it?'
'Yes, it was easy. You just have to swap LT and RT every time.'

Working with Logo provides many opportunities for the intuitive understanding of transformation geometry and other mathematical concepts. Of course children also need to learn formal definitions. They must know about order of rotational symmetry and centres of enlargement. In Chapter 8 on microworlds we will describe how we have tried to use Logo to forge a link between the equally important intuitive and formal aspects of mathematics.

Explicit mathematics

In the previous sections we have given many examples of topics from mathematics which children meet implicitly, and in Chapter 6 it will be shown how children use mathematical processes in the same way. But there are also occasions when mathematics is studied explicitly at the keyboard. It has always been one of our personal aims to create a classroom where children who are engaged in mathematics decide to use Logo to help to solve a problem or to pursue an investigation. This is not an easy goal to achieve, because it requires some degree of sophistication on the part of the children. It is much more likely in the early stages that children will suffer some mathematics if they think it will help their Logo work. Alternatively, if the mathematics and the Logo are associated in the children's minds, they may use ideas from the mathematics curriculum to stimulate Logo projects.

An example of this is provided by Daniel, who was learning about the construction of equilateral triangles in his mathematics lessons. His Logo program allowed the user to decide how big the triangle was to be, and then the construction was drawn on the screen (Fig. 5.15). The

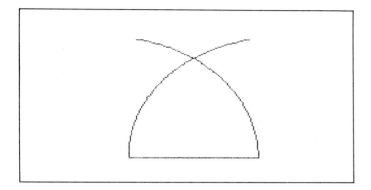

FIGURE 5.15   Example of Logo used to illustrate geometry: the construction for an equilateral triangle

program was quite sophisticated, but it is not at all clear whether Daniel's Logo work contributed in any way to his understanding of the mathematics.

Another example of a Logo project being stimulated by mathematics was the frequency chart shown in Fig. 5.16, which was drawn by Sevita and Arifa. The children did not make great advances in their mathematical understanding while drawing this chart, but they were probably consolidating

some of their knowledge. The children were using Logo to express some mathematics, and there are not very many vehicles around which allow this to happen.

We sometimes offered the children explicit mathematical ideas for Logo projects. The mathematics theme for Open Day at the school was to be 'gambling and chance', and so it seemed a good idea to suggest that children might want to write a Logo program which used the RANDOM procedure. A five-minute introduction to the whole class was enough to explain that RANDOM 5 would tell the computer to choose 0, 1, 2, 3 or 4 and to say that anyone who was looking for ideas might like to think about something which involved probability. There were three projects which developed from this. One of them was Daniel's horse race, which was described in Chapter 2. Another was a simulation of a fruit machine, and the third was a dice game written by Richard and Michael.

ONE, TWO, THREE etc. were the procedures to draw the various faces of the dice (Fig. 5.17), and RANDOM was used to determine which one would be called:

```
TO DICE
    MAKE "FACE 1 + RANDOM 6
    IF :FACE = 1 [ONE]
    IF :FACE = 2 [TWO]
    IF :FACE = 3 [THREE]
    IF :FACE = 4 [FOUR]
    IF :FACE = 5 [FIVE]
    IF :FACE = 6 [SIX]
END
```

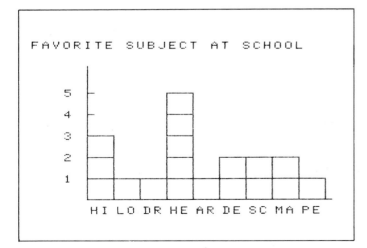

FIGURE 5.16   Example of Logo used to draw a frequency chart

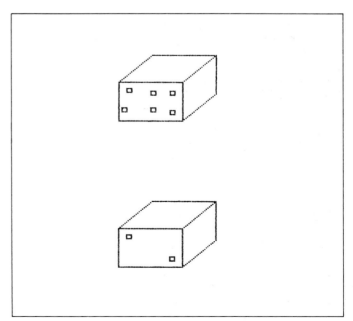

FIGURE 5.17   Example of the result of a procedure using RANDOM for a dice game

The fruit machine simulation was written in a similar way to Richard and Michael's DICE, but it had sub-procedures such as APPLE and LEMON which drew small pictures of the fruits. For each play three fruits were drawn. This led the designers of the fruit machine to consider the probabilities of combinations of events when they wanted to devise a scoring system.

Another mathematical topic which we introduced to some of the children was sequences. It is fairly simple to produce a sequence of numbers in Logo:

```
TO SEQUENCE "NUMBER
    PRINT :NUMBER
    SEQUENCE :NUMBER + 4
END
```

Typing SEQUENCE 4 will produce the multiples of 4, and SEQUENCE 17 generates the sequence 17,21,25,29,... . The children were invited to form their own sequences by changing the numbers and also by altering the last line of the procedure. Sometimes we provided them with a number of different sequences which they had to generate on the screen.

The set of sequences formed by adding a number, and then dividing by another number, is particularly worthy of further study.

```
TO SEQUENCE2 :NUMBER
    PRINT :NUMBER
    SEQUENCE2 (:NUMBER + 5) / 2
END
```

In the case above, the limit of the sequence is 5. What happens when the numbers in the last line of the procedure are altered? Can you generalise? This sort of investigation will be described in Chapter 6, and so will Daniel's work when he generated sequences by taking the square root of the previous number.

Not only can mathematics be used explicitly within Logo, but it is also feasible sometimes to use ideas from Logo to introduce some new mathematics. Children who are familiar with Logo are bound to understand the concept of variables more readily if it is presented using examples of Logo procedures with inputs. Reference to the computer will also be helpful with the general idea of a mathematical formula. A question such as 'What is the perimeter of a square of any size?' is much more accessible when it is phrased as 'How would you teach the computer to calculate the perimeter of a square? What would you need to tell the computer about your square, and what would the computer do with this number?' In the following section we will outline how the idea of the turtle can be used to gain a better understanding of directed number.

Directed numbers

The movement of the turtle along a number line can provide a helpful model for the addition and subtraction of whole numbers. This model will not necessarily suggest itself naturally as the children work with Logo, but teachers may want to refer to it when they teach the topic of directed number. All numbers and operations are represented as movements of the turtle, and the important words in the model are POSITIVE, NEGATIVE, PLUS and MINUS.

A positive number is represented as a simple movement in the direction in which the turtle is facing, so POSITIVE 7 is equivalent to the turtle moving FD 7 (Fig. 5.18).

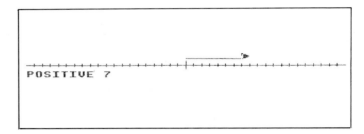

FIGURE 5.18 Procedures used to illustrate the addition and subtraction of directed numbers: POSITIVE 7 (+7)

The negation of a number or expression is defined as a (right) turn of 180° followed by the number or expression, and then a (left) turn of 180°. NEGATIVE 6 is represented by the following three commands: RT 180 FD 6 LT 180 (Fig. 5.19).

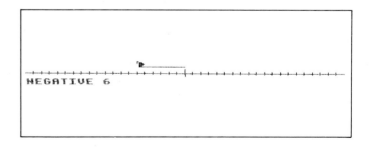

FIGURE 5.19 Procedures used to illustrate the addition and subtraction of directed numbers: NEGATIVE 6 (−6)

Addition and subtraction are modelled as the combination of two movements. The addition of two numbers or expressions is represented by their cumulative effect, so

NEGATIVE 3 PLUS NEGATIVE 2 is equivalent to the operation NEGATIVE 3 followed by NEGATIVE 2. The turtle's steps are RT 180 FD 3 LT 180 RT 180 FD 2 LT 180. The overall movement is the same as RT 180 FD 5 LT 180, or NEGATIVE 5 (Fig. 5.20).

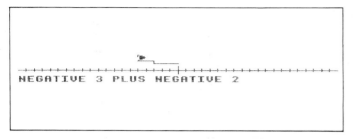

FIGURE 5.20   Procedures used to illustrate the additon and subtraction of directed numbers: NEGATIVE 3 PLUS NEGATIVE 2 ((−3) + (−2))

Subtraction is defined as the first number or expression followed by the negation of the second. POSITIVE 5 MINUS NEGATIVE 2 is equivalent to POSITIVE 5 followed by the negation of NEGATIVE 2. The turtle moves FD 5 RT 180 RT 180 FD 2 LT 180 LT 180, and the overall movement is the same as FD 7, or POSITIVE 7 (Fig. 5.21).

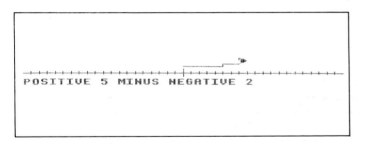

FIGURE 5.21   Procedures used to illustrate the addition and subtraction of directed numbers: POSITIVE 5 MINUS NEGATIVE 2 ((+5) − (−2))

Children can start to work with the model by playing turtle for various expressions like POSITIVE 4 PLUS NEGATIVE 5. The question they need to address is 'Which simpler expression would have the same overall effect?' They can also draw the sorts of diagrams above, and later they can try more complicated expressions which need brackets. Eventually they will meet expressions which are written in the more conventional way, such as 4 − (3 − 2 + 1), and the following rules will need to be made explicit:

1 You can use + and − instead of PLUS and MINUS.
2 You can leave out the word POSITIVE.
3 You can type −4 instead of NEGATIVE 4.

4 A negative sign in front of brackets means that the complete expression in the brackets must be negated.

This model of the number line provides a powerful way for children who are familiar with Logo to understand the behaviour of integers. In contrast to some other models which many teachers use, all numbers are regarded as movements along a number line. In order to obtain the full power of the model, it is important not to compromise this basic feature. Unfortunately, this means that the model cannot be used for multiplication, since it is meaningless to multiply two movements. There are two further points to bear in mind with this model. Firstly, the addition of two numbers cannot be considered as a single movement from a given starting position. Secondly, the negation of a number cannot be considered as a backward movement, since such an inter-pretation would not support the negation of an expression.

We have written a Logo program to drive the turtle according to this model. The program uses Logotron Logo for the BBC computer, and we will be happy to give away copies on receipt of a disc. The software is not very useful, however, apart from a short demonstration when the children are starting. A more valuable alternative might be to let the children try to produce some software for themselves. To do this they will certainly need to understand the model.

Tessellations

It was described in an earlier chapter how some children drew wallpaper patterns by defining the motif as a procedure, repeating this procedure to draw a row and, having defined the row, repeating that to fill the screen. The more able could refine this idea to draw tessellations, in which it is critical where the individual motifs are positioned so that they fit together.

A class of bright 12-year-olds were in the unusual situation of having just three sessions of Logo in the computer room. Some months earlier they had had a ten-week block, in which they had developed their own projects, but now there was not enough time for this to happen easily. The children needed some direction, and their teacher decided to focus on tessellations. The children were told that they could either define a shape, and draw it repeatedly, or concentrate on drawing the lines. The children all chose the first option. Most of them planned their work by drawing a sketch in their books, and those who finished early went on to shade their tessellations by repeatedly drawing straight lines.

The efficiency of the programs varied enormously. Some consisted of just a few lines of code, and others covered pages. All the children gained a great deal from having to convert their sketch into a computer program. Drawing a tessellation is one thing; but instructing a computer precisely where to draw each shape is quite another. Some examples are shown in Fig. 5.22.

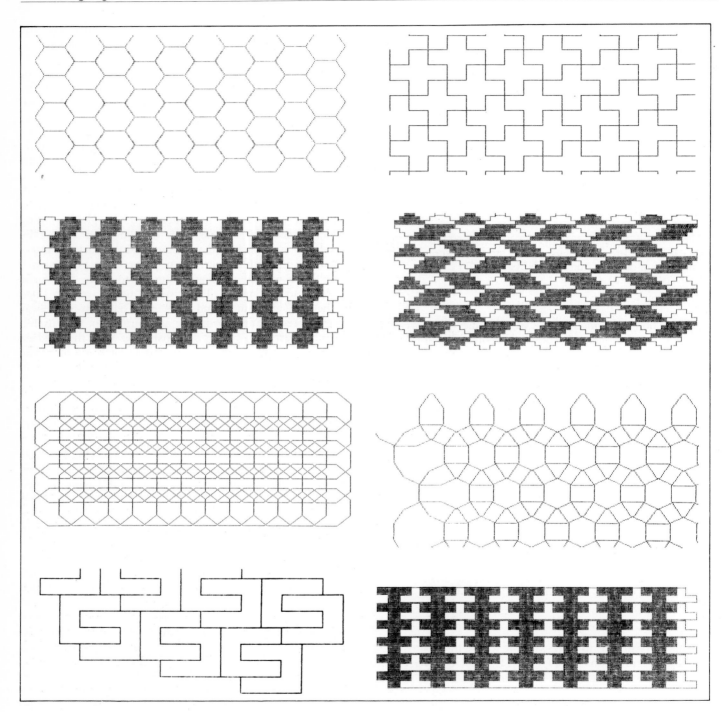

FIGURE 5.22   Examples of tessellations drawn with Logo

6 Mathematical Processes

In the previous chapter we considered many of the mathematical topics which arise when children learn Logo. We also discussed how it was sometimes feasible to introduce mathematical ideas explicitly. In this chapter we will turn our attention to the processes of doing mathematics. Here too, we will look at those processes which occur spontaneously during Logo activity, and we will give examples of mathematical investigations in which the children have used Logo to pursue their work. First of all it will be helpful to make some general comments about an investigative approach to mathematics.

Investigation is the most sophisticated form of mathematical activity. Children engaged in investigative work will be solving problems and also posing and amending problems. They will be doing practical tasks and working empirically. They will need to cooperate with other children and to discuss various approaches as they explore. When children investigate an area of mathematics, they are doing much more than simply memorising techniques for solving stereotyped problems. Children who investigate do mathematics of their own. They are mathematicians rather than the learners of other people's mathematics.

This is an approach to education which has always been practised in arts subjects. Young children paint their own pictures and write their own stories. As they get older, the emphasis of their work may change. In their art lessons they may learn about perspective, and so there will be constraints imposed on their thinking. In English lessons, more time will be given to the study of classic novels and poetry, with less attention paid to the children's creativity.

In mathematics lessons the approach has always been the other way around. All young children are required to learn many standard techniques. The ones which have become standard have often been determined by the ease with which they can be formally assessed. It is only the more able children, who go on to study mathematics at university, who are given opportunities to think for themselves in an open and creative way, and this often does not happen until the post-graduate stage. Mathematics courses at all levels should foster the processes of mathematical thinking, and many school teachers need to consider a more balanced approach.

It is generally agreed nowadays that mathematics education should contain a certain amount of problem solving and investigative work. The Cockcroft Report, *Mathematics Counts*[1], drew attention to some of the areas in which traditional teaching methods were not creating a good learning environment and outlined the key features which the authors felt all mathematics teaching should include:

- exposition by the teacher
- discussion between teacher and pupils and between pupils themselves
- appropriate practical work
- consolidation and practice of fundamental skills and routines
- problem solving
- investigative work.

Since *Mathematics Counts* was published there have been other authoritative publications, such as *Mathematics from 5 to 16*[2], which have positively recommended a more child-centred and less rigid approach to the teaching of mathematics. At the same time, much in-service work for teachers has concentrated on investigations, and many good ideas for starting points have become available: see for example *Points of Departure*[3]. The growing awareness of the importance of involving pupils in problem solving and investigative work has also been reflected in the GCSE examinations. These have put emphasis on the mathematical processes as well as the content, and they have a coursework element which encourages classroom discussion and project work.

In the following sections we will discuss some of the processes of problem solving and investigation, and we will describe how they occur spontaneously in Logo. Later on we will look at some particular investigations which children have done with Logo.

Defining the problem

When the approach to mathematics is investigative, children are not always in a position to plunge into a new problem. In his renowned book *How to Solve It*[4], George Polya talks about the need to understand a problem before a plan can be devised. A problem may need to be simplified or broken down into more manageable parts. It may be helpful to find an analogous problem which is more familiar. More generally, children need to learn to pose, amend and extend problems as well as to solve them.

Faced with the question of how many squares of different sizes there are on a chessboard, one approach might be to simplify the problem. It may be sensible to ask how many squares can be found on a smaller 2×2 board or a 3×3 board.

Even if this does not lead to a direct solution to the problem, this process allows the solver to start. Before a system has been evolved, the actual chessboard is unmanageable. There are too many squares to count them all without being confused. With a 2×2 board most children will quickly realise that there are 5 squares, and on a 3×3 board there are 14 (Fig. 6.1).

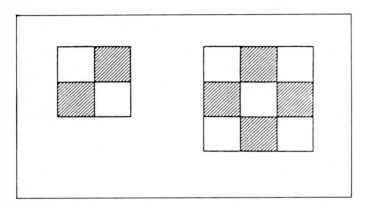

FIGURE 6.1   Small chessboards used to help to solve the problem of the total number of squares of all sizes on a normal chessboard

Physically counting the squares on these smaller boards may help the children to break the problem down. On the 2×2 board, they will have counted four 1×1 squares and one 2×2 square. On the 3×3 board there are nine 1×1 squares, four 2×2 squares and one 3×3 square. Once this has been articulated, the problem is virtually solved.

These two processes, simplifying unmanageable problems and breaking problems down, are extremely valuable. There are many mathematical problems where they are of great benefit.

The Tower of Hanoi (Fig. 6.2) is a puzzle in which the eight

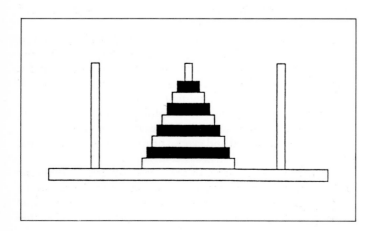

FIGURE 6.2   The Tower of Hanoi

discs have to be transferred from one of the pillars to another. The discs have to be moved one at a time, and at no stage can a disc be placed on top of a smaller one. It is not easy to solve this puzzle, and it is clearly very helpful to start with a simpler version in which there are only two or three discs. An associated problem is to find the minimum number of moves, however many discs are being transferred. Here again, a sensible way to tackle this problem is to start by actually counting the moves in the simple cases. This may lead to a pattern in the answers, or better still it may shed light on a general, analytical approach.

Many pure mathematical problems concern the effect of a situation which is determined by more than one parameter. These can often be simplified by considering the parameters one at a time. For instance, children might be asked to explore the areas of the shapes which can be created on a pinboard. In the example in Fig. 6.3, there are eight pins on the perimeter of

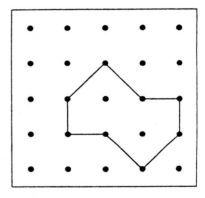

FIGURE 6.3   A shape on a pinboard with 8 pins on the perimeter, 2 pins inside and an area of 5 squares

the shape, two pins inside, and the area is 5 squares. To find some general relationship, the children will need to keep one of the variables fixed first of all. A sensible approach might be to start by collecting results for shapes which all have two pins inside.

There are many other examples from mathematics in which problems can usefully be simplified or broken down. To find the mean of the set of numbers 101, 104, 100, 102 and 104, it is much easier to work with 1, 4, 0, 2 and 4, and then to add 100 to the answer. Other problems which involve statistical data may benefit from some sort of graphical representation; looking at a problem from a different perspective often provides a way forwards. The same is true in Logo, and one of the nicest examples we have comes from a boy who wanted to simulate the movement of a car. As explained in Chapter 2, it is difficult to create realistic effects without sprites, because the computer takes too long to draw and re-draw anything as complex as a car. The solution offered by the boy was to keep the car stationary and to make a lamp-post move behind the car instead.

In fact it is not all that easy to find obvious examples like this one, in which a problem has been simplified in Logo. But the idea of breaking problems down is present all the time. Concepts like modularity, sub-procedure and top-down planning will be discussed in detail in Chapter 7, and they are all based on the central idea of breaking problems down. When Daniel and Anthony drew their wallpaper pattern on the screen (see Chapter 2), they broke the grid down into a number of rows, each one followed by a move to the start of the next. Similarly the rows were decomposed into a number of motifs, each one also followed by a short move.

In order to emphasise the skills which Daniel and Anthony brought to this problem, we will briefly describe an attempt at a similar project made by Darren and Jim when they had far less Logo experience. Their first step was to take the turtle to the top-left corner of the screen, where they wanted to start drawing:

```
TO START
   PU FD 350 RT 90 BK 600 PD
END
```

This would have been fine but, since they did not appreciate the value of modularity, they added to this procedure the instructions to draw the motif, which was an octagon:

```
TO START
   PU FD 350 RT 90 BK 600 PD
   REPEAT 8 [FD 30 RT 45]
END
```

The next step was to move the turtle, ready to draw the next octagon, and so they added a third line, PU FD 100 PD, to START. When Darren and Jim tried to REPEAT the procedure called START, the first octagon was drawn in the correct position, but the others appeared in all the wrong places.

The boys realised that the first line of START should not be repeated, and so they removed it. The next problem was caused by the fact that they then used recursion to draw the row of octagons:

```
TO START
   REPEAT 8 [FD 30 RT 45]
   PU FD 100 PD
   START
END
```

The procedure was still called START, and that tells its own story. The boys had no clear idea of the function of anything they were writing. They had not broken their problem down in the way that Daniel and Anthony had done.

Daniel and Anthony had seen the grid as a number of rows, and they had seen each row as a number of motifs. The

decision about where actually to start drawing was taken at the end, and their thinking had not been confused by it.

What Daniel, Anthony, Darren and Jim did all have in common was the fact that they had posed their problems themselves. Toward the end of this chapter we will describe how we have tried to encourage children to ask questions and to pose problems in pure mathematics, but it is not easy. Children cannot be expected to investigate mathematics unless they do this willingly, and it has to become an everyday activity. Our approach to Logo has undoubtedly been a major force in this direction, because the children's projects have all been their own.

The children all started by drawing because that is all they knew about. As they progressed to more difficult projects, they would often want to try things well beyond their capabilities, and so they had to moderate their ideas. Two children once told us that they were going to write a space invaders game. If other computers could do it, why couldn't theirs? We did not reject the idea, but the children soon realised that they had to choose something more realistic.

Even in the very early stages there were examples of children changing their goals. Suman's house started out as a castle, but he changed his goal when it suited him. Two other children who were drawing a house added a chimney to fill the gap when the roof failed to meet one of the walls. These are only small examples of the way children amend their problems as they are working. The tasks they face are not rigid ones imposed by teachers. The approach to problems in Logo which we want to encourage is more like that in a real situation. If we do not have the knowledge or the correct tools to hammer a nail into a wall where there is a concrete lintel, we hang the picture somewhere else.

As well as posing and amending problems, children should learn to extend them sometimes. Having successfully worked out that the number of squares on a chessboard is $8\times8 + 7\times7 + 6\times6 + \ldots + 1\times1$, there are obvious extensions. How many rectangles are there on a chessboard? How many squares are there on a rectangular board? How many rectangles are there on a rectangular board? The problem of the area of the shapes on a pinboard can be extended to an isometric board, on which the pins are laid out in a triangular array.

Again it is difficult to give particular examples of this in Logo because it happens all the time in a natural way. The children are always trying to extend their projects so that they achieve something which they could not do before.

Conjectures

When a mathematician finds a pattern of some sort that she can use to predict further results, she is making a conjecture. If a child is exploring the number of regions which can be obtained by joining points around a circle (Fig. 6.4), she may notice that an extra point seems to lead to twice as many regions. The child may then make a conjecture that a circle with five points will have 16 regions, and six points will generate 32 regions. The

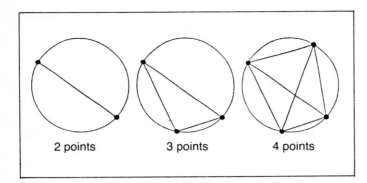

FIGURE 6.4 Patterns which could easily lead to a conjecture for more than 4 points

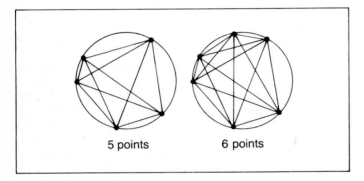

FIGURE 6.5 Development of Figure 6.4 refuting the conjecture

next stage, of course, must be to test the conjecture by drawing the appropriate diagrams (Fig. 6.5). The five-point circle runs true to form, but the six-point circle only has 31 regions. Our faith in patterns is so strong that many children will be quite sure that they have miscounted, but once they have accepted that 31 is correct, they will need to modify their hypothesis somehow. If a new conjecture does stand up to the tests which are applied, and it appears to be correct, the final mathematical stage is to prove that it will always work, no matter how many points there are around the circle.

Apart from the final stage of proof, there are clear parallels to this process in Logo, or indeed in programming in any computer language. To write a procedure is to make a conjecture; to run the procedure and to observe its effects is to test the conjecture; and when all is not well, to de-bug the procedure and then to edit it is to amend the conjecture. In the remainder of this section we will expand on these activities and explain why programming in general, and Logo in particular, provides a powerful medium for them.

When children make a conjecture by writing a Logo procedure, they are teaching a machine to do something which it could not do before. Every teacher knows that one of the best ways to understand something is to teach it to someone else.

But people have a way of interpreting what is being said to them. They read the gestures and the facial expressions as well as the words. The intonation of the voice is important and things judged to be obvious are not articulated. At times all this will help their learning and at other times it will not, but the important point here is that the machines are dumb, and they cannot interpret the commands they have been given.

A computer has no knowledge of what the programmer is attempting to do, and so the children are compelled to use precise, unambiguous and formal language. Logo will not allow the children to make assumptions. The children respect this obligation because they understand that it is not an arbitrary imposition. (Will computers still be valuable in our classrooms when they can be addressed informally, by the spoken word?) When children teach an idea to a machine they have a purpose, which may be lacking otherwise. Communicating with a machine gives a reason, a real reason, for fomulating algorithms.

A conjecture which is made in the form of a computer program is usually an algorithm. Algorithms are methods or procedures for doing something. Mathematical definitions are often written in terms of properties. For instance, a square can be defined as a shape with four equal sides and four equal angles. An algorithmic definition is equally valid, and a child familiar with Logo might define a square as the shape obtained by moving forwards a certain distance and then turning right through 90°, four times.

The procedural definition is more concrete, and the same is true when conjectures or theorems are presented in the form of algorithms. Pythagoras' theorem states that the square of the length of the hypotenuse of a right-angled triangle is equal to the sum of the squares of the lengths of the other two sides (Fig. 6.6).

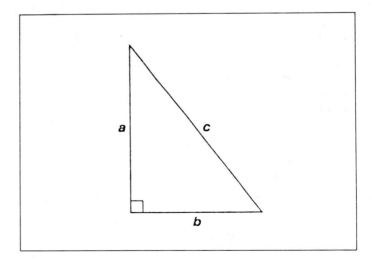

FIGURE 6.6 A picture of a right-angled triangle for illustrating Pythagoras' theorem ($a^2 + b^2 = c^2$)

The algebraic expression may be more compact and less ugly than the English language version, but it is even more abstract.

$$a^2 + b^2 = c^2$$

An algorithmic statement of the theorem is more accessible:

To find the length of the hypotenuse of a right-angled triangle, follow these three steps.
1 Square the lengths of the two shortest sides.
2 Add the results of step 1.
3 Take the square root of the result of step 2.

This algorithm could easily be presented either as a flow-chart or as a computer program.

School mathematics syllabuses have always been full of algorithms, but Logo offers the opportunity for children to make conjectures by writing their own algorithms, rather than just learning standard processes for adding two fractions or multiplying two decimals. Writing an algorithm is bound to lead to a very full understanding of the subject matter.

In Chapter 1 we described how Kim and Rupa used Logo to create an algorithm for calculating percentages. The girls had been playing a game which demanded an informal understanding of percentages. They knew that 5% meant five pennies in every pound, but no algorithm had been provided for evaluating X% of $£Y$. During the course of the game the girls had used different strategies for different questions:

What is 17% of $£3$?
  ...17% of $£1$ is 17p
  so 17% of $£3$ is 17p $\times$ 3 = 51p

What is 15% of $£56$?
  ...1% of $£56$ is 56p
  so 10% is $£5.60$
  so 5% is $£2.80$
  so 15% is $£5.60 + £2.80 = £8.40$

The game had not required any formal recording. The calculation was all done mentally, and the understanding was intuitive. A week later, however, when the girls wrote a Logo program to calculate percentages, they were forced to find one algorithm which worked in every case. This was the outcome of their efforts:

```
TO PER "PERCENT "AMOUNT
   PRINT :PERCENT * :AMOUNT / 100
END
```

Readers should not be misled by the simplicity of this final procedure. The result took over an hour to achieve because the girls had to create the definition for themselves. During their struggles, Kim and Rupa made many conjectures. Each time they tested the conjecture by running their procedure, and then, when it proved to be false, they amended it by using the editor. At one point during the lesson they produced this procedure.

```
TO PER "PERCENT "AMOUNT
   MAKE "ONEPER :AMOUNT / 100
   PRINT :PERCENT / :ONEPER
END
```

As soon as it had been completed, the girls naturally tested it. They typed PER 2 50, and when the computer printed the number 4 on the screen they were not too sure. On typing PER 10 20, and seeing 50 on the screen instead of 2, they realised that something was wrong. The next stage was to study their algorithm and to try to locate the error. When this version of the procedure was written, the girls had been exploring, and the feed-back offered by the computer had encouraged them to proceed.

Would this mathematical process have occurred without the computer? The answer must be that it is far less likely that it would. Pencil and paper provide a useful tool for recording. But they do not always encourage an exploratory approach. They do not necessarily suggest any activity. The computer keyboard, in contrast, begs to be used. One only needs to catch the slightest glimpse of an appropriate procedure, and it seems perfectly natural to key it in and try it out. (In fact, children are so prepared to explore possibilities that teachers may have the reverse problem of having to persuade them to stand back and reflect occasionally.)

When an algorithm has been programmed incorrectly (or when an incorrect algorithm has been programmed), the computer gives fast and reliable feed-back on the programmer's efforts. Children are continually comparing the actual outcome of a procedure with the outcome which they had intended. At the same time, the computer does not expect the programmer to respond in any particular way, and so it is far less threatening than a critical human being would be. Some bad examples of educational software have overwritten this positive feature of the computer by creating situations in which certain anticipated responses must be entered before the child can progress. In fact, some computer-assisted learning packages have gone even further, and the child's response is timed. When they are working with Logo, the children can be sure that the computer will exercise infinite patience while they discuss what to type next.

Kim and Rupa could test their conjectures regularly by running their latest version of PER. Another important feature of their work, which is closely linked to this, was their positive attitude to the errors they made. This will be discussed more fully in the following section, and we will leave the last words of this section to some Logo learners. Firstly there is a paragraph from Kim.

'The problem was to devise a program that could work out percentages efficiently. What it does is if you write PER and two numbers, e.g. PER 2 100, the answer would come up as 50. It *sounds* easy doesn't it?!!

'The program is quite a simple one but it took quite a lot of thinking . . . It was a bit hit and miss the way we worked it out. First of all we thought if you divide two numbers together you get the percentage, but it isn't that easy. Ronnie came over and helped us a bit so we got the idea and after a bit of arguing we got it all sorted out.'

The remaining paragraphs were written by two students who were intending to become teachers. We have omitted most of the technicalities in order to emphasise the algorithmic nature of their work. They showed amazing persistence as they created, tested and amended various conjectures.

'Our first problem was in drawing the clock hands as we could not have two hands moving round due to there only being one turtle. So we started off by trying to draw one hand, erase it, turn the turtle to a different angle and draw the hand again in a new place.

```
TO BIGHAND
    FD 110 BK 110
    PE FD 110 BK 110
    RT 6 PD
    BIGHAND
END
```

We told the turtle to turn right 6° because that is equivalent to the space of one minute.
'We repeated the procedure, with modifications, for the little hand. The little hand must move on 0.5° each time in order for it to have moved 30° in the same amount of time that it takes the big hand to move 360°. This would then move like a real clock.
'However, the turtle only drew the big hand, continuously repeating the procedure BIGHAND, because we had not told it when to stop and move on to LITTLEHAND. We should have had another procedure which told the turtle to draw first the big hand and then the little hand:

```
TO HANDS
    BIGHAND
    LITTLEHAND
    HANDS
END
```

In order for the turtle to do this, the last lines of BIGHAND and LITTLEHAND have to be deleted.
'However, when we tried this program we realised that what the computer was in fact doing was drawing the big hand then moving the turtle round 6°, drawing the little hand in that position and then moving the turtle round 0.5° and drawing the big hand from there. In effect what we saw on the screen was one hand appearing and disappearing, moving round the screen.
'Next we decided to separate the two procedures in a different way, having one command to draw the hands

and a second to tell the hands to move on . . . This, however, did not work as it moved the hands round at a constant angle to each other, and those on a real clock would not be.
'We next tried drawing the little hand, then moving the big hand 12 times so it supposedly rotated 360°, before moving the little hand on to the next hour . . .
'All in all the procedures did not work, so we tried a new approach. The idea was to have a main procedure and two sub-procedures for the big hand and the little hand. So the turtle moved on to the two sub-procedures, then returned to the main procedure which would inform the turtle of the new angles to draw the hands at.
'After this the program did in fact work . . .'

Working systematically

All scientists need to work systematically at times, and the mathematician who is solving a problem is no exception. The solutions of many of the mathematical problems discussed in this chapter have required a systematic approach. The notion of working systematically is quite general, and it does not necessarily suggest any specific actions. For this reason it is a good idea for children to have the phrase in their minds as they tackle mathematical problems. We recommend that children are taught to question regularly whether or not they might be able to improve their strategy by working more systematically.

When Afzal wanted to find the correct angle to draw a regular heptagon (seven sides) on the screen, he made good use of a more methodical approach. His work was described in detail in Chapter 5, but we will refer to it again here, together with other examples of children's Logo which have less explicit mathematical content.

Afzal's first strategy was trial and error. He tried REPEAT 7 [FD 100 RT 50], and when he found that an angle of 50° was too small, he tried something bigger. The everyday phrase 'trial and error' implies a fairly haphazard approach, based on guesswork. This may be the case, but trial and error can also be systematic. The important feature is that subsequent trials should be based on previous errors. Many of the advanced techniques of numerical analysis are essentially trial and error methods, and it is worthwhile for children to use this approach too.

When children start to use Logo, drawing pictures often involves trial and error. If they are drawing an outline, the last line will need to join up with the first, and the children might have to estimate its length. Floor turtles leave a noticeable spot on the paper when they are stationary, and young children's drawings often show tell-tale signs of trial and error methods (Fig. 6.7). If the children are confident, they may raise the turtle's pen so that they can overestimate without drawing and then, when they know the length in question, they will go back and draw the line.

Hilary and Carol were excited by drawing circles, and they used trial and error to design a caterpillar (Fig. 6.8). Their first

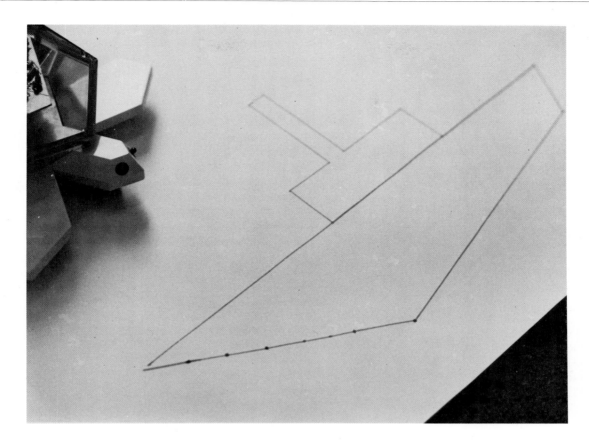

FIGURE 6.7   A floor turtle and a child's picture

attempt at a circle was to type REPEAT 30 [FD 15 RT 10]. The circle was not complete and so they used the same command again, without clearing the screen. This did give a complete circle, but it was still not satisfactory because the girls were not then able to position the turtle correctly for the second circle. They needed to get the turtle to draw a complete circle, without retracing its path. They cleared the screen and tried a similar command with the number 30 replaced by 35. The circle was not quite complete, and so they used 37. This time the turtle moved slightly too far, and so they settled for REPEAT 36 [FD 15 RT 10].

We do not have any records to show how they drew the five circles for the caterpillar's body. They may have programmed the turtle to draw one and a half circles each time, but it is also feasible that they typed PU (pen up), turned through 90°, and then used trial and error again to find the diameter of the circle.

When the body was complete, Hilary and Carol needed to draw the head. This was also a circle, but it had to be smaller than the ones they had already drawn. They could have reduced the number 15 so that the turtle did not move so far forwards each time, but their first inclination was to alter the angle. They changed it to 5, but they found that the command REPEAT 36 [FD 15 RT 5] only drew a semicircle. The

obvious answer was to try REPEAT 72 [FD 15 RT 5]. This circle was too big and so, rather than halving the angle, they decided to double it. It was at this point that their work involved a more analytical approach. They recognised that there was a relationship between the angle and the number associated with REPEAT. When the angle was halved the number was doubled, and it seemed a reasonable bet that doubling the angle would mean that the number had to be halved. They typed REPEAT 18 [FD 15 RT 20], and it worked.

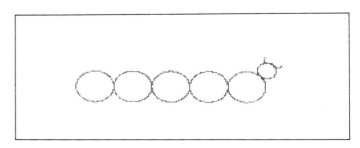

FIGURE 6.8   A caterpillar constructed from circles produced by trial and error

The product of the two numbers in question must always be 36Ø. Afzal also noticed this pattern while he was working with regular polygons. (In fact the problems are identical because the circles which Hilary and Carol were drawing were actually polygons with a large number of short sides.) In both cases the children had moved on from trial and error methods to finding patterns and relationships, and this is another mathematical process which is connected with a systematic approach.

Writing Logo programs, children learn to look for patterns in their code all the time. Young children who want to draw a circle will start by playing turtle themselves. When they appreciate that they need to make small movements and small turns, they may type FD 1 RT 1 FD 1 RT 1 and so on. This is obviously quite tedious, and so the children will be encouraged to notice the pattern in the commands they are typing and to use REPEAT.

If there are more than two commands which repeat, it may be sensible to write another procedure. For instance a child who wants to draw a staircase across the screen might start with a single procedure containing a long list of commands:

```
TO STAIRCASE
   FD 1Ø RT 9Ø
   FD 1Ø LT 9Ø
   FD 1Ø RT 9Ø
   FD 1Ø LT 9Ø
      .
      .
      .
```

A recognition of the pattern in this code will save a lot of typing. The child needs to write a sub-procedure for the two lines which repeat:

```
TO STAIR
   FD 1Ø RT 9Ø
   FD 1Ø LT 9Ø
END
```

This can then be used within STAIRCASE:

```
TO STAIRCASE
   REPEAT 2Ø [STAIR]
END
```

We will end this section by discussing the systematic process of de-bugging which children must learn from Logo. When children start to use Logo, they are often heard blaming the machine when its response is unexpected. They transfer the responsibility for an error to something that cannot answer back. As the children progress it becomes less common to hear someone call their machine 'stupid'. They learn, instead, to re-examine their own work. Errors are very common when writing a computer program, just as they are when any creative work is being undertaken. Programs hardly ever work exactly as they were intended the first time, and the search for bugs is an essential programming activity.

Children learn to de-bug by working through their programs systematically. They might play turtle by walking around the classroom, or they could trace the turtle's path mentally or on paper. RML Logo has a WALK command, which enables the computer to execute a procedure one step at a time. Since it is so easy for the children to edit their work in Logo, they learn not to be easily discouraged. In fact the search for bugs is often seen as an exciting challenge. The emphasis is always very firmly on how to get things working properly the next time, rather than on what went wrong last time. This short poem by Piet Hein says it all:

The Road to Wisdom
The road to wisdom, well it's
plain and simple to express
err
and err
and err again
but
less
and less
and less

The stigma which is normally associated with errors is considerably lessened while programming a computer. Pencil and paper have a more permanent feel than a monitor screen, and the children are often afraid that they will do something wrong and have to start again. When wrong algorithms are written on paper, the bugs are not always quite so evident. The same mistakes that were made when the algorithm was created are often repeated when it is used. Testing algorithms on paper is a chore, and it is hardly surprising that we tend to cut corners. School children are often told to read through their finished examination scripts to check for mistakes. Unfortunately, they do not often find very many because they make the same mistakes again. It is not a chore for a child to run a Logo program which she has written. That is what it is all about.

The last part of this chapter will be used to describe some mathematical problems and investigations which children have pursued with Logo.

Spiral patterns

One of the starting points which features in many publications concerns the spiral patterns which can be made from sequences of numbers (Fig. 6.9).

We used the notion of the turtle, but not the computer, to explain the rules to the children. We wrote the sequence 1, 2, 4 on the overhead projector, and we drew the turtle's path for the commands FD 1, RT 9Ø, FD 2, RT 9Ø, FD 4, RT 9Ø. This sequence of commands was repeated until the turtle was retracing its steps, and the diagram was complete.

The children experimented for some time using pencil and squared paper with different sequences of numbers. Despite

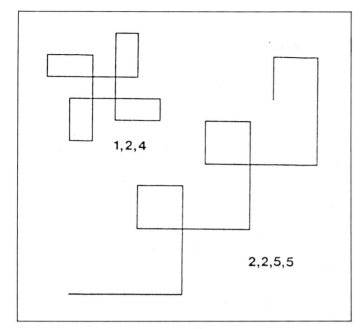

1,2,4

2,2,5,5

FIGURE 6.9   Spiral patterns produced by sequences of numbers

the use of the imaginary turtle, there was still one boy who turned left instead of right occasionally, but with some extra attention he managed to produce the correct diagrams.

After 40 minutes or so, we invited the children to ask some suitable questions about the work they had been doing. This is a technique taken from *Generating Mathematical Activity in the Classroom*[5], which is designed to encourage the children to explore their own directions and to ask their own questions. We wrote up all the children's questions on the overhead projector.

- Do you get the same pattern if you subtract 1 from each number in any sequence?
- Do you get the same pattern if you double each number?
- Does it matter if the order of the numbers is changed?
- Do consecutive numbers always give the same pattern?
- Do the patterns always repeat themselves?
- Can you get the same patterns from different numbers?
- When does the pattern spiral off the page, and when does it return to its starting position?
- Does the number of numbers tell us anything about the patterns?

The list is impressive, but it must be borne in mind that not all the children contributed, and we often helped the children to articulate their thoughts. Nevertheless, the list was then used to provide a focus for further activity. The children were still free to follow their own directions, but here was a number of explicit questions which the children could address if they wanted to.

During the remaining 30 minutes of the lesson, the children pursued many of these questions, and they made many discoveries. The next lesson was in the computer room with Logo. We had hinted that the children might want to follow up their investigation, but we certainly did not force any of the children to abandon other projects if they did not want to. Four children did use Logo to generate the spiral patterns.

Annabel and Ann wrote a procedure called LINES:

```
TO LINES
    FD 10 RT 90 FD 20 RT 90 FD 40 RT 90
END
```

When they typed REPEAT 4 [LINES], the complete pattern appeared on the screen. Anil and Clyde wrote a procedure called SPIRAL. This was the same as LINES, except that it called itself recursively at the end. This meant that SPIRAL was sufficient to draw the pattern, but the turtle did not stop when it was complete. It continued to move, indefinitely.

It was early in the year, and the children had not worked with Logo for very long. Annabel, Ann, Anil and Clyde changed a few numbers here and there, and looked at the different patterns, but they did not have the expertise in Logo to be able to substitute the values of 90 in their programs for a variable and then to test the effect of changing the angle. They did not use their Logo programs to draw any specific conclusions. They had not yet acquired the problem solving skills necessary to explore systematically. They did not look at several patterns of the same form and generalise from their observations. At least they did not do these things explicitly. The fact that they were writing a computer program about a mathematical topic, and then observing the effects of their program, must have improved their understanding of the problem to some extent.

The children were quite happy with their work. They had not set out to make startling mathematical discoveries. Logo had been their motivation, and they were pleased to have been able to draw the patterns from their mathematics lessons on the computer screen. In our experience, when children link Logo and mathematics, the mathematics often provides a good starting point for some interesting Logo work. It is not so common that the children want to go back to the mathematics. The Logo captures their imaginations, and the mathematical ideas are understood in less explicit ways.

WHIZZ

The spiral patterns investigation was introduced to the children away from the computer. The use of Logo may have been suggested, but there was no compulsion for the children to use their Logo time to pursue the mathematics. It may be tempting to take a firmer line sometimes, and this section will be used to describe the problems we faced when we tried to do just that.

Our aim had been for the children to work mathematically with a procedure which we had written. We had produced a

---

Logo WHIZZ

Type this procedure

```
TO WHIZZ "SIZE "ANGLE
   FD :SIZE
   RT :ANGLE
   WHIZZ :SIZE :ANGLE
END
```

WHIZZ draws patterns: it needs 2 variables.
Try typing WHIZZ 100 40
Press ESC to stop whizzing round the screen.

What does WHIZZ do?
What happens if you change the numbers?
Do all the shapes join up?
Do they cross over?

What makes a shape bigger?
What changes the shape?
What makes the shape go off the screen?

Can you WHIZZ a square?
A star?
A rectangle?
A circle?

Can you classify the shapes?

FIGURE 6.10   The worksheet used for the WHIZZ investigation

worksheet for the children to use, and it contained a number of questions as well as providing a way to get started (Fig. 6.10).

In their mathematics lessons the children were accustomed to engaging in some activity which was presented to them and then thinking of suitable mathematical questions which might be posed. We had hoped that the same lesson format would work in the Logo room. The children were told in advance that the next lesson would be rather different, and that they would not be working on their own projects, but there was still much resistance. Even before the lesson had started, Clyde complained: 'Do we have to do that WHIZZ today?' Undaunted by this, we distributed the worksheets and asked the children to explore different inputs for 10 or 15 minutes, with the intention of collecting questions afterwards.

After a very short time most of the children had become quite bored, and so they rid themselves of the constraints we had imposed. They started to alter the procedure itself. They added colours, and they inserted new commands. Two children even altered the last line of the procedure so that the value of SIZE was incremented, and spiral patterns were drawn.

In one sense, of course, this was all very well. After all, the children were only doing what we normally expected them to do in their Logo work. But it was now impossible to stop the lesson and to collect the children's questions. We had hoped to have been bombarded with questions such as "Can you get a star with 19 points?" and "Which numbers give stars and which numbers give regular polygons?"

Why did the lesson fail? Some children were not excited enough by the patterns. They had seen stars before. Another factor which must be of some significance was the environment. The children had different expectations in the different rooms where they were taught. In the ordinary classroom they expected to follow our starting points, whereas in the computer room they did not. They were used to working on their own projects, in which they set the goals. WHIZZ was presented to the whole class, and it was seen as an imposition. Perhaps the most intrusive aspect of all was the fact that the actual procedure was written for the children. We had offered other mathematical topics by suggesting an idea, such as a game of chance or a tessellation design, without writing anything for the children, and this had been much more successful.

In general, the message seems to be that teachers cannot have their cake and eat it at the same time. If Logo is to offer all the educational benefits of independence, ownership and control, we cannot also expect the children to work at our problems.

POLYSPI and INSPI

It is with all the reservations of the previous section that we will now describe two procedures which have become Logo standards. Every text about Logo seems to have a section on the breath-taking patterns (not to be confused with those of our earlier section on spiral patterns) which are produced on the screen. These designs are so easy to create with Logo that nearly all the children are likely to want to explore them at one time or another.

POLYSPI is actually very similar to WHIZZ, the only difference being that each line is drawn longer than the one before:

```
TO POLYSPI "LENGTH "ANGLE
   FD :LENGTH
   RT :ANGLE
   POLYSPI :LENGTH+5 :ANGLE
END
```

As with WHIZZ, the variable called LENGTH is not of much interest. In WHIZZ it determined the length of each line, and here POLYSPI 20 90 produces a pattern in which the first line to be drawn is 20 units long. The quantity :ANGLE is the one which can be varied to obtain such exciting results (Fig. 6.11). All the questions on the WHIZZ worksheet apply to POLYSPI, but the patterns are more exciting, and so the motivation to investigate is stronger.

POLYSPI 20 90

POLYSPI 0 71

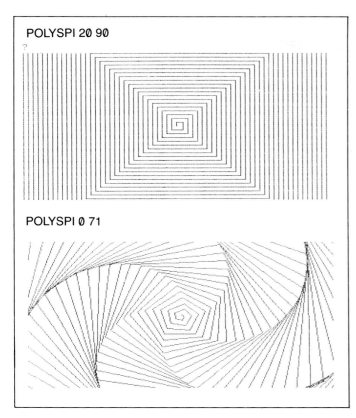

FIGURE 6.11   Patterns produced by incrementing a variable in POLYSPI

INSPI 50 0

INSPI 20 2

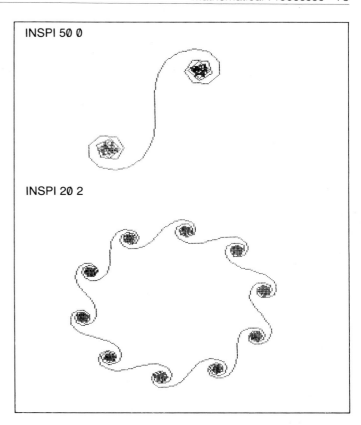

FIGURE 6.12   Patterns produced by incrementing a variable in INSPI

The POLYSPI procedure can be altered so that it is the angle which is being incremented, rather than the length.

```
TO INSPI "LENGTH "ANGLE
    FD :LENGTH
    RT :ANGLE
    INSPI :LENGTH :ANGLE+5
END
```

Here, the patterns are more complex (Fig. 6.12). Again, the variable LENGTH is insignificant, and it is interesting to study the different designs which can be obtained by changing :ANGLE. However, in the INSPI procedure the variation of the increment also provides an activity with much mathematical potential. This can be written into the procedure:

```
TO INSPI "LENGTH "ANGLE "INC
    FD :LENGTH
    RT :ANGLE
    INSPI :LENGTH :ANGLE+:INC :INC
END
```

See Fig. 6.13 for two examples of this modified version of INSPI.

POLYSPI, INSPI and WHIZZ are all really black box procedures. Provided that the children understand how they work, there is not too much to be gained by looking inside them or altering them. The main purpose of working with them is to investigate the effect of running the procedures with different values for the variables. This classroom activity is more like that associated with much computer-assisted learning software than the open Logo work described in this book. This is not to suggest that it is inappropriate; only that teachers need to be aware of the expectations of the children when these procedures are being used.

Square roots

We will end this chapter on a more positive note by describing another investigation which we introduced away from the computers, and which a few children pursued with Logo. This was a study of the sequences of numbers generated using the idea of square root. We had already been using trial and error methods to find the square roots of numbers: "Which number gives 30 when it is multiplied by itself?" The children had used calculators to find better and better approximations. 5.4×5.4 was less than 30, and 5.5 was too big, so they tried 5.45 . . .

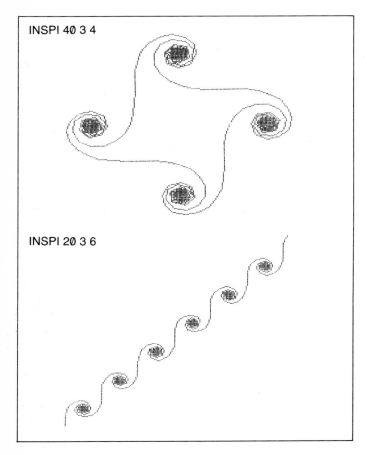

INSPI 40 3 4

INSPI 20 3 6

FIGURE 6.13   A development of the INSPI procedure

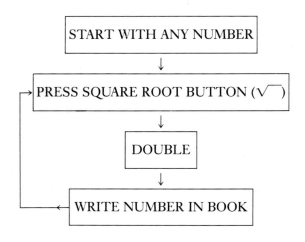

FIGURE 6.14   Flowchart used for an investigation of square roots

This activity had given the children a better understanding of place value and decimal notation, and it served as a good introduction to the investigation we will describe here.

The problem (Fig. 6.14) was to find out what happened to any number when the square root was doubled, and the same process was applied to the answer, indefinitely. The whole class began using 39 as the starting number:

```
39
12.489995
 7.0682374
 5.3172312
 4.6118244
 4.2950316
 4.0718012
        .
        .
        .
```

At the end of their first lesson with the exploration, most children had gone through this process four or five times, and they were fairly sure that the answers would always get closer and closer to 4, no matter what the starting number was.

Daniel came back after school that day, and decided to write a Logo program to produce the sequences of numbers. Daniel often used Logo after school as he waited for his father to collect him, and it is clear that his main motivation was an opportunity to program the computer, rather than an interest in the pure mathematics.

None of the children in the class had done any non-graphical work at this stage, but Daniel had seen the procedure SQRT (square root) described in the handbook. Given some help with the correct form of MAKE, Daniel wrote a recursive procedure which he called ERS:

```
TO ERS "D
  MAKE "E SQRT :D
  MAKE "F :D * 2
  PRINT :F
  ERS :F
END
```

ERS could have been written more elegantly, without MAKE:

```
TO ERS "D
  PRINT :D
  ERS 2 * SQRT :D
END
```

But Daniel did not ask about style. His procedure worked, and that was what mattered. When he typed ERS 39, the computer quickly produced the same sequence of numbers that he had taken many minutes to work out with his calculator. In fact the computer generated more numbers than he had bothered to do, and after a short period the numbers which were scrolling off the top of the screen were all the same, i.e. 4.

Daniel was justifiably pleased with his achievement, and so we talked about how he might improve it. The first obvious amendment was to insert a command which made the procedure stop at the right time. This did not involve any new mathematics for Daniel, since he already knew that the answers would get closer and closer to 4. He added the line IF :D=4 [STOP] at the beginning of his procedure.

The next suggestion did lead to some new mathematics. Could Daniel alter ERS so that it would cope with trebling, or multiplying by 5, instead of doubling? This might lead to a generalisation of the original problem. Daniel produced the following amended version of ERS by replacing the 2 with a variable:

```
TO ERS "D "S
  IF :D=4 [STOP]
  MAKE "E SQRT :D
  MAKE "F :D * :S
  PRINT :F
  ERS :F :S
END
```

Daniel could now type ERS 40 7, and the computer would generate a sequence of numbers, starting with 40, and successively taking the square root and multiplying by 7. Daniel had generalised successfully, but at the same time as he solved one problem, he unsolved another. The stopping condition no longer worked, and the numbers scrolled off the screen again as they had done before he inserted the conditional line. The numbers generated by ERS 40 7 do not get closer to 4. The limit of the sequence is actually 49, and so the recursive process did not terminate.

Daniel realised what the problem was, but it was not at all clear how he would deal with it. He might have noticed that the limit was always the square of the multiplier, in which case he could have changed the first line to IF :D=:S*:S [STOP]. Alternatively, he could have tested each sequence for the equality of two successive terms: IF :D=:F [STOP]. In fact he did not take either of these steps. It was time to go home for tea, and in the next lesson with the computers Daniel continued his racing car project with his partner.

As with the spiral patterns, it may not be so important that Daniel did not express a mathematical formula explicitly while working with Logo. Even though he did not write an expression such as :D=:S*:S he did learn somehow that the limit would always be the square of the multiplier. When we casually asked him what he thought would happen if he typed ERS 117 6, he promptly replied that the numbers would approach 36, and Daniel had not appreciated this before his Logo session.

In Chapter 1 we quoted a teacher who was worried that, if her children spent time working on their Logo projects, they would not be able to get through everything on the mathematics syllabus. We hope that the last two chapters have illustrated how much mathematics children do learn from their Logo, but the teacher may still have doubts. Most of the mathematics is not explicit, and secondary teachers in particular may find it hard to reconcile this with the obvious demands of the syllabus. We cannot hope here to address all teachers and all the different contexts in which they are working. We are not in any position to argue a political case for Logo. However, the educational arguments are clear to us. We would describe the activity of programming a computer as applied mathematics. Our experience tells us that children who learn Logo are doing mathematics of some sort all the time, and that they are getting mathematical experiences which they would probably not get in other ways.

In the primary school and at the lower end of the secondary school, there may be problems of finding sufficient hardware to allow a reasonable number of children sufficient access to the machines. However, the work which has been described in these chapters must surely provide justification for the mathematical value of Logo. The constraints of the syllabus get greater as the children get older. Examinations at 16+ have often discouraged teachers from providing Logo and other rich experiences, but the new GCSE examinations offer more opportunities. They put more emphasis on extended coursework, and on process as well as content, so that Logo projects could easily become part of the coursework element in mathematics.

7 Structured Programming

In this chapter we will discuss some of the key ideas of structured programming in Logo. As in the other chapters of this book, our main emphasis will be to offer as much practical help as possible to teachers who are using Logo, and so we will give plenty of space to the sorts of problems which children often face. This book does not aim to provide a tutorial for learning Logo, and we will assume that you know what terms like 'sub-procedure' mean. If this assumption is wrong, there are plenty of books around which do teach Logo as a programming language. Alternatively, you would learn more by asking someone else, and then using a computer to explore the idea for yourself. However, we will give an overview of the concept of sub-procedures before we discuss the children's difficulties in learning about them, and we hope that this might help you to link some ideas which you may not have connected before.

We have not tried to cover every aspect of the Logo language in this chapter. The use of inputs is omitted, because the concept of variable has been discussed in Chapter 5, and more advanced topics, such as output, recursion and list processing, are missing, because we do not know enough about how children learn them. With Logo the use of procedures naturally encourages a structured approach, and so it is important for teachers to be aware of the main ideas at an early stage.

Sub-procedures

The full power of procedures can only really be appreciated when they are designed to be used within other procedures. Programs are written in Logo by using the primitive commands as building bricks and combining them in various ways. The combinations are also building bricks, which can be combined, and so on. A sub-procedure can be called (used) once or several times within a program.

When procedures are linked, it is necessary to be aware of their full effect. Children may use PU (pen up) in a procedure to move the turtle without drawing any lines. When their procedure has been executed, however, the turtle's pen will remain up, and this may catch some children out. There is no problem when the procedure is used on its own, but when it is a sub-procedure the turtle may have to execute another one when this one has finished. The subsequent procedure may have been tested independently after typing CS (clear screen). CS restores the turtle to its original state, with the pen down, and so the picture will be drawn without any problem. After the PU command has been used, however, the turtle apparently wanders about aimlessly and nothing is drawn.

The process of a sub-procedure is important, as well as its product. In turtle geometry it is often just as necessary to know where the turtle starts and finishes as it is to know what will be drawn. The RML Logo command to write a procedure is BUILD, whereas LCSI and MIT have used TO. These words imply that procedures are seen as nouns and verbs respectively, and this highlights the two different aspects.

Rashid and Alan had drawn a jet. Its nose was at the top left-hand corner of the screen, and its tail was in the opposite corner. Perhaps it was taking off; it was certainly climbing. They had written a procedure, so that when they typed JET it would be drawn on the screen. At the same time, Lois and Raje had been exploring patterns. They noticed that one of their results looked quite like a picture of the night sky, and so they wrote it as a procedure. At the start of the following lesson, the boys heard about SKY, and they asked the girls whether they could use it as a background for their aeroplane. They loaded their file and also the girls' file, so that they could use both procedures. SKY worked without any difficulty, but when they typed JET the aeroplane was drawn upside-down, with only half of the plane on the screen. Until this point in their learning, the boys had only associated the word JET with the one drawing which they wanted. They had always used the procedure with the screen blank, and the turtle starting at the centre, in the home position. After having executed SKY, the turtle was in a different place, and so typing JET had a different effect.

Children who are writing a procedure sometimes asked us where the turtle will be at the start. This is not an easy question to answer. 'It depends where it is at the time!' and 'It depends where you left it!' are fairly inadequate responses. However, the question itself shows that the children are starting to think about the process of the procedure.

Modularity

A conceptual development of the use of sub-procedures is the ability to write in a structured, modular style. The class teacher in Chapter 1, who asked all the children to draw the same shape (Fig. 7.1), was hinting at this, and the two more experienced children did produce a program which was modular.

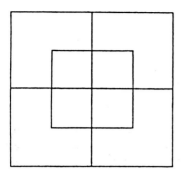

FIGURE 7.1   Design which children were asked to reproduce with Logo: relationship to the concept of modularity

```
TO SHAPE
   REPEAT 4 [SQUARES RT 90]
END

TO SQUARES
   SQ 50
   SQ 100
END

TO SQ "SIDE
   REPEAT 4 [FD :SIDE RT 90]
END
```

The children's approach had been to draw the two squares which form a quarter of the shape four times. The main procedure, which they typed to run the program, was SHAPE, and this instructed the computer to repeat its sub-procedure SQUARES, turning the turtle through a right-angle after each call. SQUARES was used to draw the two squares of different sizes by calling SQ twice, and SQ did the job of actually telling the turtle to draw each square. In contrast to this, two other children wrote a long, unplanned list of commands. Their single, linear procedure was quite unwieldy, and they must have had a hard time de-bugging if it did not work smoothly at first. Modular programs are made from a number of procedures, which each do one small task. Typically these procedures are short, and their function is clear. They are more difficult to produce than linear sequences of commands, and children will need plenty of time to learn how to write them effectively.

Top-down planning

The more experienced children in the previous example planned the structure of their program in advance. They adopted what is called a top-down approach. This means that their thinking, and possibly their typing, started with the biggest problem, the complete design, and they considered how to break it down into smaller problems. Before they had written any code, they decided that the shape was to be made from four quadrants. They may have then defined the procedure called SHAPE at the keyboard. SHAPE calls SQUARES as a sub-procedure, which they had not yet written, and so they would not have been able to test SHAPE immediately. Next, in a similar fashion, they designed and wrote SQUARES, using the as-yet undefined SQ as a sub-procedure, and finally they wrote SQ.

This approach to programming is not typical of children who work with Logo, but it might suit some. Others will be happier with a bottom-up approach, in which they plunge in somewhere with a procedure that they can write fairly easily, and then build up more complex procedures from it. In the adult world of business and industry, there are some occasions when a top-down approach may be appropriate. It may be that the program can be specified in all its detail in advance, and the programmer has written comparable programs before. However, there are also times when a more creative, bottom-up style is called for. When a programmer is also concerned with the design of the program, she is likely to think of further ideas as she progresses. When the program is half finished new possibilities may suggest themselves. An uncompromising top-down approach would stifle such initiatives.

State transparency

A procedure is said to be state transparent if the state of the turtle remains unchanged after it has been called. The phrase itself is ugly, and not particularly helpful, but the idea is a valuable one. In a state-transparent procedure the turtle finishes in the same place as it started, and also with the same heading. Both of the procedures below will draw the same square, but SQ1 is state transparent, whereas SQ2 is not:

```
TO SQ1
   REPEAT 4 [FD 100 RT 90]
END

TO SQ2
   FD 100 RT 90 FD 100 RT 90 FD 100 RT 90
   FD 100
END
```

SQ1 is much easier to work with than SQ2. If a picture or a pattern is made from a number of squares, it would be much harder to keep track of the position of the turtle with SQ2. With SQ1, the programmer can position the turtle, draw the square, and then be confident about the turtle's subsequent position. The two children who wrote their program in a structured way, above, wrote three procedures, SHAPE, SQUARES and SQ, and each of them was state transparent. In fact, a top-down approach almost obliges the programmer to use state-transparent procedures. It may be an interesting, academic exercise to try to re-write the three procedures, replacing the state-transparent SQ with SQ2.

Learning about structure

It is important for teachers to be aware of the ideas of structured programming, but there are not very many children below the age of 14 or 15 who are able to understand them in an abstract way. Many children who want to draw a square will use a procedure like SQ2, and there is no point in insisting that they make it state transparent, unless they can appreciate the purpose. The process cannot be rushed, because they will certainly not see any reason for state transparency unless they have had plenty of time struggling with procedures like SQ2. The example above of the design made from squares is not typical. The task was too easy for the children in question, who were extremely bright, and they were able to plan their complete program before they used the keyboard. In fact there was not very much point in these children using the computer at all for this task. They could have done it just as well with paper and pencil.

One of the reasons why Logo is so accessible is the fact that children can start to program before they have learned the more sophisticated and abstract ideas. Logo is a highly structured language and, in general, children working freely will learn to exploit that structure when they need it. The ideas of modularity, top-down planning and state transparency are not easy for children, but the following account of a project shows how two children did learn to think in a more structured way as the need arose.

Annabel and Leena drew a computer keyboard on their screen (Fig. 7.2). The squares represent the keys and they have letters drawn in them. The children had started with a procedure called KEYBOARD, which was originally intended to draw the whole thing. They had completed one square (for the letter G), and moved on to the next one, when they realised that they would need to repeat this process, and so they decided to finish their definition of KEYBOARD:

```
TO KEYBOARD
  FD 30 RT 90 FD 30 RT 90 FD 30 RT 90 FD 30
  BK 30
  PU BK 15 PD RT 90
END
```

FIGURE 7.2   A representation of a computer keyboard

Then they wrote another procedure, KEYS, to draw a row of squares and to move the turtle back to the start of the top row:

```
TO KEYS
  REPEAT 11 [KEYBOARD]
  PU FD 45 LT 90 FD 495 RT 90 PD
END
```

Their final procedure for the keys was called KEYS2, and this does the remaining task of drawing the top row of squares:

```
TO KEYS2
  REPEAT 11 [KEYBOARD]
END
```

In their main super-procedure, called HANDYCOMPUTER, the girls cleared the screen, drew the rectangle, and then called KEYS and KEYS2. There is nothing wrong with Annabel and Leen's work so far. In fact, they have shown far more understanding of modularity than most of the children of their age. The point we want to emphasise is that this structure developed as the girls were typing. It was not thought out in advance. They were learning about modularity.

This can be seen even more clearly in the procedures for printing the letters. LETTERS gets the turtle to the right place, and then it starts to print the letters themselves. However, after printing Q and H the girls finish this procedure, even though it was initially intended to print all the letters. Note that the girls were using RML machines, and the procedure called LABEL is a primitive which prints letters (or words or lists) at the position of the turtle. This is not available on most computers, but we have left it in this transcription to LCSI:

```
TO LETTERS
  PU LT 90 FD 480 LT 90 FD 30 LT 90 PD
  SETPC 2
  LABEL [Q]
  PU FD 45 PD
  LABEL [H]
END
```

At this point, having printed two letters, Annabel and Leena noticed that the penultimate line of their procedure, which served to move the turtle from one square to the next, would be needed several times, so they wrote another procedure to do this particular job:

```
TO LETTERS1
  PU FD 45 PD
END
```

They did not change anything that they had written, but their new procedures incorporated LETTERS1 as a sub-procedure.

```
TO LETTERS2
   LETTERS1
   LABEL [T]
   LETTERS1
   LABEL [I]
   LETTERS1
   LABEL [F]
   LETTERS1
      .
      .
```

Annabel and Leena learned a great deal about structuring their procedures while they were working on this project, but it is also clear that they still have some way to go. If they were writing LETTERS2 now we would want to encourage them to alter LETTERS1 first of all, so that it incorporated the LABEL command:

```
TO LETTERS1 "MESSAGE
   PU FD 45 PD
   LABEL :MESSAGE
END
```

They could then make LETTERS2 much shorter, because all the LABEL commands would be unnecessary:

```
TO LETTERS2
   LETTERS1 [T]
   LETTERS1 [I]
   LETTERS1 [F]
      .
      .
```

LETTERS2 is still long and unwieldy. All its commands are similar, and it can be made much neater and more flexible with recursion:

```
TO LETTERS2 "MESSAGE
   IF EMPTY? :MESSAGE [STOP]
   LETTERS1 FIRST :MESSAGE
   LETTERS2 BF :MESSAGE
END
```

All that is necessary now is to type LETTERS2 [T I F . . .], and the computer will execute LETTERS1 for each item in the list. The use of recursion with lists is more advanced than most of the work described in this book, but this example does illustrate two things. Firstly, it shows how more structure can be developed from the children's work when it is appropriate. Whatever the children are doing, there is nearly always scope for a teacher to intervene, if she wants to make some suggestions. At the same time, there will also be plenty of ideas which the teacher may see, but which are not appropriate for the children at that particular stage. In the following section we will describe a game which can give the whole class a better understanding of the structure of a Logo program.

The Procedure Game

Children should be provided with good models for Logo programs, and when there are several procedures which refer to each other, they need to understand the flow of control so that they can de-bug them successfully. A game which has been designed for this purpose involves a group of children, with one child acting the part of each procedure.

When we played the Procedure Game with children, we started by distributing the sheet shown in Fig. 7.3.

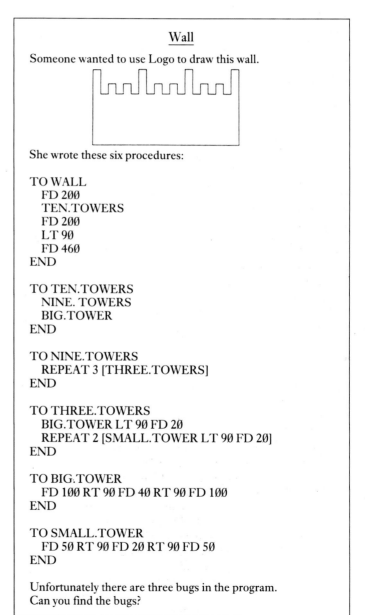

Unfortunately there are three bugs in the program. Can you find the bugs?

FIGURE 7.3   Worksheet for use in the Procedure Game

First of all we invited the children to spend five minutes finding the bugs on their own. One or two children had some ideas but they were not certain, and they realised that it was not an easy task. We then set about dry-running the program, using an overhead projector to trace the turtle's path. We wrote the name of the super-procedure, WALL, at the foot of the screen, as if someone had typed it at the keyboard, and then we invited a child to step forward. This first child had to be WALL, and so we gave her a card with the word on it, for her to hold. While WALL was being called she had to stand up, and she also had to take the projector pen to execute any turtle commands in her procedure.

WALL read her sheet and drew the vertical line from the first command. Her next instruction was TEN.TOWERS, and so another child had to stand up and take the pen from WALL. It was most important at this point that WALL did not sit down. She had only executed two of her five instructions, and her job was not yet complete. Even though TEN.TOWERS had the pen now, WALL was also still being called. When TEN.TOWERS was complete she would have to return the pen to WALL, who would then be able to finish her instructions.

In fact TEN.TOWERS did not use the pen. She immediately passed it on to NINE.TOWERS, but again she had to remain standing until her job was complete. The same process continued all the way through the program, each child standing to execute the instructions in her procedure, performing any turtle commands at the overhead projector, and then sitting down and returning the pen when the procedure was complete.

The game lasted about 20 minutes the first time we played, but later on we played whenever we had some time to fill. Children who could not find the bugs were of course free to type the program at their computer during a subsequent lesson. At the keyboard the problems were usually resolved quickly. When one solution did not work, the children could try another. However, we wanted the children to play the game away from the machines, so that they were forced to think about the flow of control in a Logo program. This does not suggest that they should physically act out every program which has a bug, but hopefully they were more able to trace their programs as a result of playing the game.

Two further points arise from this game. Firstly, we only acted out the six procedures which the programmer had written, and we ignored the primitive procedures. If the game is taken to its logical conclusion, different children should stand up and play the part of FD, LT, RT and REPEAT each time they are called. In our view this would have made the activity too long and involved for the children, but it might be more appropriate at a more advanced level.

The other feature we did not introduce was procedures with inputs. Again, this becomes more important at a higher level, especially when the children need to understand full recursion. This procedure is an old favourite for catching out Logo learners.

```
TO REVERSAL "NUMBER
   IF :NUMBER = 1Ø [STOP]
   REVERSAL :NUMBER + 1
   PRINT :NUMBER
END
```

What is the effect of typing REVERSAL Ø? (The name of the procedure should give you a clue.) REVERSAL will be called 11 times altogether, and it will have a different input each time. Before she writes anything on the projector, REVERSAL Ø has to pass the pen to REVERSAL 1 and remain standing. When the pen is returned to her, later in the process, REVERSAL Ø will have to finish her job by writing Ø on the projector. The inputs are critical and so it is a good idea to have cards for them too. As REVERSAL Ø passes the pen to REVERSAL 1, she should also give her a card with the number 1 written on it, to slip in her pocket.

While this game is valuable, it is hardly ever possible for a teacher to describe a child as having 'understood' modularity. Sub-procedures, modularity, state transparency and top-down planning are some of the powerful concepts of Logo, which take a long time to develop. Logo is a practical activity which allows this development to happen in a fairly natural way. When children first meet a new idea, they will not generally have any kind of overview, and even though they may have understood it in someone else's program, they may not be ready to put that idea into practice for themselves. Children often work with an incomplete understanding, and this is illustrated in the following section.

Incomplete understanding

In conventional school subjects, especially mathematics, children are often given new concepts in a simplified form so that they can digest them more easily. Unfortunately, this often means that the concept itself is not conveyed properly. In a Logo environment this is unlikely to occur, but there are other difficulties which arise when new concepts are learned in a natural way. The children often work with an incomplete understanding of their work, because the 'noise' has not been removed artificially.

When the children in our classes wanted to learn how to get the computer to ask a question and then to respond to the answer which is typed, we gave them a sheet with this procedure on it:

```
TO SPEECH
   PRINT [WHAT IS YOUR NAME?]
   MAKE "REPLY RL
   PRINT [ ]
   PRINT FPUT "HELLO :REPLY
END
```

The children needed some time to explore SPEECH because it contained other new ideas, apart from RL. Firstly, the procedure called MAKE may not have been seen before. RL (readlist) asks for the input from the keyboard, but there is no point in having the computer find out the user's name unless it stores the response in its memory somehow. MAKE has two inputs; firstly the name of the store, and secondly the contents of that store. The use of lists, and FPUT in particular, is also probably new for the children at this stage. FPUT (put first) forms a new list with "HELLO at the start of the list :REPLY.

MAKE and FPUT can both be considered as 'noise' as far as the understanding of RL is concerned. This means that a child may have to start working without understanding everything fully, but in the long run her conceptual understanding will be firmer it she has had to deal with the knowledge in a proper context. In the example above, we presented the new procedures, noise and all, to the children. There are also many examples of misconceptions which arise without apparent intervention from the teacher.

Lois was learning Logo on a BBC micro, and *. is one of the commands which has to be used on this computer. It is not actually a Logo command at all, but it is necessary to type *. if you want to see a list of all the files on the disc. The command to get one of the files from the disc is LOAD, and for a long time Lois thought that *. had to be typed first if LOAD was to work successfully. She knew the name of her file perfectly well, but she still insisted on seeing a list of all the files before she loaded her own. We are not certain why Lois had this misconception, and we can only assume that she saw her teacher, or another child, typing the two commands in succession, and she did not realise that they were independent. Lois did not have any difficulties, and she certainly did not ask for help over this matter, but her understanding of the functions of the two commands was incomplete, and this may have held her up in the future.

A similar example, but in a more important conceptual area, concerns Michael. He had drawn a boot, which he wanted to make smaller, and so he was introduced to the idea of variable with the suggestion that he divide each length in his procedure by a variable amount:

```
TO BOOT "SIZE
  FD 200 / :SIZE
  RT 90
  FD 100 / :SIZE
  RT 90
  FD 300 / :SIZE
  .
  .
  .
```

This worked perfectly well, and Michael could draw his boot in different sizes. He certainly did not have a full understanding, however, because, when he wanted to draw a square of variable size, he continued to use division:

```
TO SQUARE :SIZE
  FD 100 / :SIZE
  RT 90
  FD 100 / :SIZE
  .
  .
  .
```

It would have been much 'easier' to use FD :SIZE instead of FD 100 / :SIZE, but Michael was not yet able to isolate the features of the BOOT procedure which were to do with variables. Just as Lois thought that *. was part of the loading process, Michael understood the division sign (/) to be something to do with variables.

Both Lois and Michael had misconceptions. There are also many examples of children who find an acceptable technique for the particular situation in which they find themselves, but one which is less than perfect in other respects. For instance, many children use HOME to send the turtle to the centre of the screen, when state transparency would provide a far richer option. Richard and Michael wrote six procedures to draw the different configurations of dots on the faces of a dice. They knew that the procedures would have to be used in various orders, and so they started each one with the sequence PU HOME PD. Later on, when they wanted to draw two dice, they came unstuck. The HOME command meant that the dots could only be drawn in one place on the screen. Had the six procedures been state transparent, with the turtle starting and finishing at the same point on the dice each time, Richard and Michael would have been able to draw the dice wherever they wanted. But state transparency is a difficult idea, and there are many other situations in which only one drawing is required, and the use of HOME is good enough.

There are many minor linguistic mistakes which occur regularly. Children often leave out important spaces between words. They type LOAD"FRED or EDIT"HOUSE. Sometimes they insert spaces which should not be there, e.g. SET MODE 7 is typed when the children really wanted to use the procedure called SETMODE. Since these are errors, the computer will reject them, and the children are forced to find the correct way to enter their instructions. The difficulties which are caused are therefore small, but they can be attributed to an incomplete understanding of the consistency of the Logo language. Spaces are most important in Logo, because they indicate where one word finishes and another starts. There are no primitive procedures in Logo by the names of SET or LOAD"FRED. Logo is a consistent language, and a rationale exists for the way words can be combined within a command, but this is not fully evident to the children, who tend to learn the various instructions in a rote way, and only discover the underlying patterns slowly.

The only punctuation signs in Logo are the quotes (") and the colon (:), and there is also a consistent rationale for the use of these. If a word is immediately preceded by quotes, then it is regarded as a meaningless string of characters. The colon is used to evaluate the variable which has the word as its name, and if a word has no sign at the beginning, it is assumed to be a procedure. Children cannot be expected to take all that in when they first meet the use of punctuation, and to make matters worse, their introduction is likely to involve arbitrary conventions. For instance, in the title line of a procedure, LCSI Logo requires quotation marks or a colon in front of the name of the input, whereas RML uses a quote (SQ 'SIZE), which is optional. No colon or quotes are required in any version of Logo when a procedure is defined (TO SQ or BUILD SQ). MIT Logo also relaxes the rule with the use of ED (edit) and ER (erase), whereas LCSI insists on the quotes, and RML Logo allows you to choose whether or not you include them with CHANGE and insists that you do with SCRAP.

In this aspect of Logo, as in so many others, the children will work for some time with little understanding of the underlying principles. Once they get past all the initial confusion, it is worthwhile for them to learn the general rationale, and so the teacher has to be continually finding opportunities for discussing this with them.

8 Logo Microworlds

Turtle geometry is an example of a microworld. The learner is provided with a safe and limited environment in which to explore. Goals naturally suggest themselves and the learner gains control and independence. The following paragraphs are used to discuss the main features and characteristics of the learning environment which turtle geometry can provide. Later in the chapter, we will look at some other important Logo microworlds, and finally we will discuss some mathematical extensions to turtle geometry.

A microworld is limited

It is clear that a learning environment must be limited in some way, so that actions and thoughts are focused. Turtle geometry allows the exploration of two-dimensional space, but it would not necessarily be a useful medium for a study of the cube. The limits of turtle geometry are defined by the objects of the environment (e.g. the monitor screen, or a turtle on the floor) and by the commands which are available (FD, RT etc.). It is important to recognise that, while the tools of the microworld are limited, the activities of the learners are not. There are very many things to do. There are many goals to achieve and many different ways to achieve them. There are also many things to learn.

The environment generates goals

A computer running Logo and a pinboard with elastic bands are two examples of learning environments. Logo provides the sort of stimulating environment in which open-ended explorations lead naturally to self-imposed goals. This is not true in the same way of a pinboard, even though there is plenty of scope for problem solving and mathematical learning. The main difficulty with pinboards is that the environment itself does not necessarily generate any valuable activity. The mathematically minded will find questions to ask, but most children will need to be directed by the teacher. Problems need to be defined clearly before any mathematical activity can happen. This is not to deny the value of a period of play when children are first presented with the equipment. Young children will happily use the elastic bands to create patterns. But such activity may eventually become aimless. Typically, this is prevented by the intervention of a teacher, who poses a particular problem or suggests some actions. The teacher will know from her experience that the problem or

actions have potential value, but this is not necessarily evident to the children.

The contrast with the turtle geometry microworld is very clear. Here, the children will start by playing with a few simple commands (FD, BK, RT, LT, CS), and the exploration of these commands will inevitably lead to goal-directed tasks which the children have set themselves. In turtle geometry there are things to do as well as things to learn. A young child will soon want to create a house or a boat, and her actions will inevitably lead to thinking about lengths and angles. The things to do provide the purpose, and it is the activity which leads to the learning. But with materials like pinboards there is not much to do until you know what you want to learn.

The activities are accessible

There is much computer software which is powerful, but the power is not always accessible. Children can derive enormous benefits from continued contact with a word processor or a database, but powerful versions are often difficult to use. It is not just that the power is not easily realised: the software itself is inaccessible without the initial mastery of many technical matters. In order to circumvent such difficulties, software designers have devised 'educational' versions. These inevitably lack power and it is likely that the children will outgrow the software.

Logo is the most powerful language which is available on today's school computers. There are several microworlds from which to choose within Logo (e.g. turtle geometry, sprites, music) and in each case only a few commands need to be provided for many activities to become accessible.

A good microworld is accessible because children of all ages can use it by being provided with some small part of it. This is in contrast to other environments in which it is not possible to engage without first having mastered many technical skills. From the outset the whole of a microworld is available to be claimed in a natural and unforced way.

Control, independence and ownership

A kitchen has many of the qualities of a microworld. If it is well equipped and well stocked a large variety of dishes can be created using a limited number of utensils and ingredients. Most people do not have too much difficulty thinking of something they want to cook. But for the beginner, an additional aid is necessary. It is not easy to start without a cookery book and someone else's recipe to follow. Of course, an experienced cook can adapt recipes, or invent her own, use seasonal foods, and alter the ingredients to taste. A novice, however, needs to be told what steps to take, and the order in which they must be taken. The apprentice cook in her kitchen microworld is not in full control of her own learning. In order to progress she needs to follow a precise path which has been determined for her by someone else. All successful learning is bound to require guidance occasionally, but a good microworld like turtle geometry does not need recipes, and so it will not force any kind of dependence.

When children own their work, it matters to them. The children are in control of their own learning, and they can make effective decisions about the work they are doing. Their satisfaction, or indeed their frustration, comes from within. Extrinsic rewards or punishments are redundant. Logo offers an environment which stimulates exploration and suggests goals to be achieved. Children can be encouraged to create projects and to develop their own ideas.

After turtle geometry?

Teachers often ask what the children do after turtle geometry, and the answer may well be rather incoherent, with some garbled references to list processing and other advanced techniques. Before we attempt to do better, let us make it absolutely clear that children should not be expected to finish turtle geometry on one day, and then start another course on list processing the next. List processing is not a microworld. It is not a subject which merits attention for its own sake, except for computer scientists. It may be possible to organise projects for children which are based on the manipulation of text, but these do not suggest themselves naturally as many projects in the turtle geometry microworld do. Also, list processing is not accessible in the same way as a microworld. Before it becomes feasible to attempt the sorts of programs that might motivate children, they will need to have mastered ideas like recursion and output. Lists are simply Logo's way of storing information. Sometimes it is necessary to manipulate this information, and that is the function of list processing. Children who write more advanced programs in turtle geometry or any other Logo microworld will stumble upon situations in which list processing is important, and this is the time when they should learn about it.

The question about children's activities after turtle geometry has not been fully answered yet. Some of the children in our classes, who spent a great deal of time learning Logo, did need some further stimulation towards the end of their year. The brighter children were able to write more advanced programs which started with the turtle. David's maze game began with long strings of turtle commands to draw the maze, but the programming skills which he used later went far beyond what most people think of as turtle

geometry. Children who could not attempt similar projects needed some new starting points other than the turtle. The provision of different microworlds allowed these children to make a 'fresh start'. They were able to bring much of their previous learning to a completely new context, and the different microworlds also created a need for the children to learn new skills and new techniques.

Control Logo

Computers are being used more and more to control other machines. In Chapter 1 we described how some children were using Logo to control a crane made from Lego bricks. Children also love to control buggies, so that they move forwards or backwards and turn around when the children press certain switches. As well as working models, children enjoy designing trap-doors for classroom pets and simulations of Pelican crossings.

This work requires a control board and extra software to provide procedures such as TURNON, SELECT and READPORT. Two such systems currently available are CLARE[1] and CONTROL LOGO[2]. CLARE has been designed so that the children can achieve many results using only the various devices on the board which is supplied. On one side of this board are a number of output devices: as well as the junction boxes where motors can be attached, there are a buzzer, a bulb, a seven-segment display and a bar of light-emitting diodes (LEDs). The following procedure makes the buzzer sound and three of the LEDs light up:

```
TO BUZZLIGHT
   SELECT "SOUND
   SENDPORT 255
   SELECT "BARS
   TURNON [2 4 5]
END
```

The devices can be switched off with the commands SENDPORT Ø and TURNOFF [2 4 5]. The recursive procedure below could be used to make the bulb get brighter and brighter:

```
TO BRIGHTER "BRIGHTNESS
   IF :BRIGHTNESS > 255 [STOP]
   SENDPORT :BRIGHTNESS
   BRIGHTER :BRIGHTNESS + 1
END
```

In order to run the procedure, the child would have to type SELECT "BULB followed by BRIGHTER Ø.

The CLARE board also has three input devices: a light sensor, a heat sensor and eight switches. READPORT is used to find out how much heat or light is entering the device. If a child wanted to design a fire alarm, she would need to turn the buzzer on when the temperature rises.

```
TO ALARM
   SELECT [HEAT BUZZER]
   IF READPORT > 150 [SENDPORT 255 WAIT 50
      SENDPORT 0]
   ALARM
END
```

The use of the IF procedure to make decisions is a natural event in the use of control Logo. The children who made the crane started by selecting "MOTORS, and then they used TURNON and TURNOFF sequentially to make the various parts of the crane move. It was then an obvious development to use the switches to determine which motors were on and which were off:

```
IF (STATE 5) = 1 [TURNON 3][TURNOFF 3]
```

This command instructs the computer to turn on motor number 3 if switch number 5 is on, otherwise to turn the motor off.

Music

Most computers have the facility to make sounds, although the range of possible sounds and their quality vary considerably, and they are not always very accessible. On the BBC machine with Logotron Logo, there are now two good software packages which make music available to many children: LOGOSOUNDS[3] and MUSIC LOGO[4]. At the time of writing, these are still quite new, and so we do not have many examples of children's work yet. In the following paragraphs any named procedures are from LOGO-SOUNDS.

The essential commands are NOTE and PLAY. NOTE has two inputs, for the pitch and the duration of the note. Thus NOTE "G 20 produces a note of pitch G, and the 20 gives a length of note that is suitable for use as a minim. A second input of 10 would then give a crotchet and 5 a quaver. PLAY enables the programmer to produce a sequence of notes. PLAY [E G B D F][5 10 10 5 20] gives five notes of differing lengths. If the duration of each one is to be the same the second input can be a number: PLAY [E G B D F] 10.

Just as turtle geometry allows children to work with lengths and angles without any formal knowledge of mathematical theorems, so these music commands enable children to produce sounds before they have mastered the technicalities of a musical instrument. Children readily explore the different notes they can achieve, and provided that they know how to write procedures it does not take long before they are ready to teach the computer to play a simple tune. The following procedure was written by Shvetu and Gareth, and it plays the theme music from *Starwars*.

```
TO L1
   PLAY [C R G F E D c G][15 2 15 5 5 5 15 10]
   PLAY [R F E D c G][3 5 5 5 15 10]
   PLAY [R F E F D R][3 5 5 5 15 5]
   PLAY [C R G F E D c G][15 2 15 5 5 5 15 10]
   PLAY [R F E D c G][3 5 5 5 15 10]
   PLAY [R F E F D R][3 5 5 5 15 5]
END
```

The letter R signifies a rest, and the lower-case c signifies a note in the next octave.

There are many further ideas for the children to explore in LOGOSOUNDS. Lower notes can be achieved, and sharps and flats can be used. Various assorted noises are also available, and all the notes and noises can be played with different voices. A chorus effect is easily obtained. The volume of the sounds can be altered, and at a more advanced level the amplitude of the voices is controlled with ATTACK, DECAY, SUSTAIN and RELEASE. There is even a command called KEYBOARD which converts the computer into a musical keyboard, so that the keys play notes directly.

There are some contrasts to be drawn between the features of a music microworld and those of turtle geometry. Obviously one is about sound and the other concerns vision, but there are some further implications to do with children's activities. Firstly, sound is transient whereas pictures are not. This means that it is not practicable to work with music at top level. The children need to write procedures if they are to achieve anything worthwhile. Provided that they are able to do this, it seems that music may encourage a structured approach more readily than turtle geometry does. When children write a tune, it often appears to be obvious to them that each line should be a separate procedure, and that the procedures can be repeated if necessary. In contrast, it may take children some considerable time before they appreciate that a row of squares is best achieved by writing a procedure for a single square first of all.

This may be because a sequence of notes, unlike a picture, is a linear entity. The children have no difficulty in converting the string of notes into a string of Logo commands, and so it is much easier to see the structure at the outset. Children who want to draw a circle may start by typing FD 1, RT 1, FD 1, RT 1 etc., and it is not until they see the commands printed on the screen that they understand their structure. Any mental image of the drawing itself was probably not helpful.

A sharper contrast between children's programming activities with music and those with pictures concerns the nature of their projects. With music they are more likely to choose an existing tune, rather than to create one of their own. Children are of course free to pursue either path, just as they are with the turtle, but for some reason the turtle encourages children to create their own designs whereas music challenges them to re-create melodies they know. The combination of this and the transparency of the structure often leads to a top-down approach when children program tunes.

Sprites

Control Logo and music are two microworlds which are independent of turtle geometry. They might be used alongside the turtle, and children do enjoy writing programs which have both pictures and tunes, for example. With the proviso that there is not very much room for exploration in direct drive, teachers have the freedom to decide whether to introduce these microworlds before turtle geometry, at the same time or afterwards. Sprites are different because they are really extended turtles. They have extra attributes which allow the children to create realistic animation on the screen.

Firstly they have a speed which can be altered with the command SETSP. When the child types SETSP 30, the sprite will continue to move until the speed is altered again. The sprite's direction is controlled in a similar way to the turtle. In addition to this a sprite's shape can be edited so that it looks like a boat or a person or whatever it is that the child wants to animate. At present the sprite facility is available on the RML Nimbus, the Atari and the BBC with Logotron Logo (using extra hardware which is costly). Sprites will certainly become more widespread as more powerful machines become cheaper.

Sprites are highly motivating, and they are used by children in a number of ways. Minesh and Shailen converted a sprite into the shape of a pencil, and then they used standard turtle commands to make the pencil draw a tree. Nasmin and Amber created a beautiful underwater landscape with seaweed swaying, sea anemones opening and closing, and fish swimming amongst the various plants. Anthony, Rizwan and Leandro wanted to make the computer play tennis. They used one sprite for each bat and another for the ball. They used the procedure called TOUCHING to detect when the ball had hit the bat, and then they changed the direction of the ball.

The possibility of detecting collisions is often useful. William, David and James designed a game where one red sprite moved across the screen, and the player used a joystick to make a white sprite jump out of its path. If the two sprites collided the game was lost, and an appropriate (!) message was printed on the screen. Other children elaborated on this theme in various ways. Shooting aliens and dropping bombs are seen as essential activities with a computer by many of the boys.

We would not want to encourage children to develop the warlike aspects of these games, but sprites also stimulate other programming projects which are unlikely to happen with turtle geometry alone. In particular, for some children the animation strongly suggests the possibility of telling a story. In one school we visited, the teacher had introduced the idea of an adventure game to the class, and many children who had started with only text on their screens went on to illustrate the adventure with sprites.

James used sprites to tell the story of Noah's Ark. It started with a picture of the ark (a sprite) on the water. Further sprites were used to depict the falling rain, and then Noah walked up the steps of the ark and disappeared. Noah was actually two sprites being shown alternately to give the appearance of a man walking. As the water rose (a normal turtle drew several straight lines), the ark moved upwards so that it appeared to be floating on the water. Finally a raven (yet another sprite) flew from the ark to the edge of the screen.

Our final example of the use of sprites was produced by Andrew and Anthony. Their program showed a javelin thrower running and then throwing a javelin into the air. When the javelin had nearly reached the edge of the screen, some trees starting moving in the opposite direction. Then they stopped, and the javelin fell to the ground.

Sprites are highly motivating for many children. They make it possible for the children to work on ideas which they have seen in the commercial games they run on their home computers. Children who use sprites can clearly aim at different goals from those who use a turtle, but we ought to express some reservations we have about using sprites too early.

Thoughout this book we have been stressing the control children develop when they work with Logo. This control comes from their identification with the turtle, and the children that we have taught knew where the turtle was and which way it was heading at all stages of their projects. It appears to us to be much more difficult to control sprites in the same way. Once a sprite has been set in motion, it continues to move, disappearing from one edge of the screen and reappearing on the opposite side. This means that it is not feasible to work at top-level, without writing procedures. Even after some considerable time with the turtle, many children need to draw their pictures at top-level, keeping a record of their commands so that they can write a procedure later. With sprites the children have to start by writing procedures, and then amending them when there are bugs.

Despite the fact that children work at different sorts of projects with sprites, the programming techniques they use are much the same. Sprites do not necessarily enhance the mathematical processes the children use or the concepts they learn. The extra motivation provided by sprites is hardly essential in the early stages. There are very few children who are not captivated by the standard turtle, and we feel that teachers would be well advised to spend any additional funds on more Logo chips, or a disc drive or a printer. Once the children have a solid base of experience with the turtle, and more time is available for Logo, then sprites may be a worthwhile consideration.

Transformation geometry

It is quite feasible to create new microworlds by extending existing ones. In the remainder of this chapter we will describe some examples of mathematical extensions which were produced in conjunction with the ATM Logo Working Group[5]. Our general aim has been to allow the children to explore mathematical ideas through Logo — to study mathematics without destroying the environment which Logo has helped to create.

TRANSFORM is software which has been written in Logo. Several procedures, such as DRAW, FLIP and ENLARGE, are provided, and these can be regarded as primitive. As far as the children are concerned FLIP is similar to FD, in the sense that both of them are a part of the Logo language.

The transformations are local to the position and the heading of the turtle. If a child writes a procedure of her own, called FLAG, she can then type DRAW FLIP [FLAG] and the turtle will execute the procedure FLAG, but all instances of LT and RT will be swapped before this happens (Fig. 8.1). The new flag will be drawn wherever the turtle happens to be.

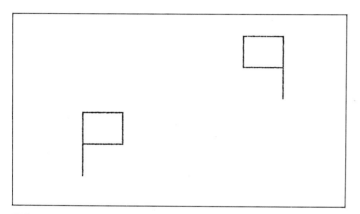

FIGURE 8.1   Illustration of the effect of the FLIP procedure

If a child has drawn a house, she might want to draw another, smaller house. Provided that she has placed the turtle correctly, she could type DRAW ENLARGE 0.6 [HOUSE] (Fig. 8.2).

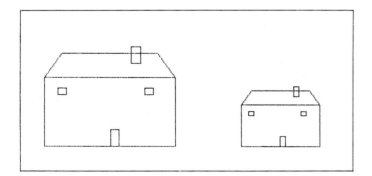

FIGURE 8.2   Illustration of the effect of the ENLARGE procedure

The transformations can be combined easily because the procedures have an output. If a child has drawn a small flower, which bends to the left, she can create a larger one which bends to the right by typing DRAW FLIP ENLARGE 2 [FLOWER] (Fig. 8.3).

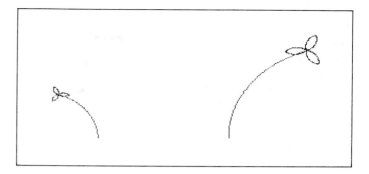

FIGURE 8.3   Illustration of the effect of combining the FLIP and ENLARGE procedures

The transformations described above are all standard mathematical ones, but some teachers may prefer to use the more general procedures from which FLIP and ENLARGE were derived. FLIP interchanges all instances of LT and RT, whereas SWAP allows any two words to be interchanged. When a child types DRAW SWAP "FD "BK [FLAG], her FLAG procedure will be executed after FD and BK have been swapped. This produces a 180° rotation of the original flag, but there are many more possibilities. Swapping PU (pen up) and PD (pen down) might have interesting results.

ENLARGE scales all the inputs to FD and BK. If HOUSE contains the command FD 20, the effect of DRAW ENLARGE 2 [HOUSE] will be to transform this command to FD 40. SCALE is more general than ENLARGE because the user can choose which words to scale. Thus DRAW SCALE 2 [RT LT] [PERSON] means that all the angles will be doubled before PERSON is executed. Using SCALE with [LT RT] does not produce a transformation which mathematicians would find useful, but it is important that children should be allowed to explore these possibilities for themselves. This way the children will learn to recognise valuable transformations. Indeed, if it is not provided for them, the children might be able to define ENLARGE for themselves by using SCALE with [FD BK].

Some children will try to use INCREMENT to enlarge their drawings. DRAW INCREMENT 100 [FD BK] [PICTURE] adds 100 to each FD and to each BK command, and in general PICTURE will be distorted. INCREMENT with [FD BK] does not preserve angles, and children are not often given any opportunity to explore various transformations in this way. Conventionally, it is far more likely that a particular transformation such as enlargement will be defined for the children and that there will be no discussion of the possible alternatives.

Another feature of the TRANSFORM software allows the user to simulate up to seven turtles. Transformations can be set between successive pairs, and a single command can be given to move each of the turtles. TRANSFORM [ENLARGE 1.2 FLIP] sets the transformation. START [0 0 0 0] 200 determines the starting configuration, and in this case there will be four turtles, each with zero heading (facing upwards) and 200 units apart from one another. On typing ALL [PU FD 100 PD BOAT], the first turtle obeys the instructions in the list. The second turtle runs the list after it has been flipped and enlarged. The new list is transformed again before the third turtle moves, and so on (Fig. 8.4).

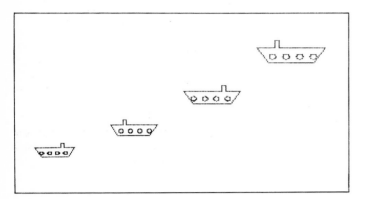

FIGURE 8.4   Illustration of the effect of the simulation of four turtles together with the FLIP and ENLARGE procedures

The mathematical transformations may be more appropriate when more than one turtle is being used. There are many questions which might arise in this situation, and it is to be hoped that the children will be stimulated to pose some of them for themselves.

'If the transformation is set to FLIP, when is the final picture symmetrical? Where is the mirror line? What sort of transformation has happened if there is no line of symmetry?'

'Using your own procedure for a flag, and two turtles, can you find different ways to draw the same picture?'

'Using two turtles, when can you force them to meet at the same spot? Or, starting at the same place, explore different paths for the two turtles.'

'If you type TRANSFORM [FLIP FLIP] the commands LT and RT will be swapped twice in each transformation, and each turtle will trace the same path. Can you achieve the same effect by using ENLARGE twice?'

'Set the transformation to INCREMENT 30 [RT] and (using four turtles) type ALL [REPEAT 12 [FD 100 RT 30]]. Investigate similar situations.'

'Can you create a wallpaper pattern or a tessellation design?'

Mathematical extensions

There is plenty of perfectly good software around which deals with transformation geometry, but the point of using TRANSFORM is to preserve all the benefits of Logo and to teach topics from the mathematics syllabus at the same time. We described in Chapter 7 how children learn mathe-

matical processes, concepts and skills while they are working with turtle geometry. The list of mathematical ideas which are inherent in Logo is a very long one, but the mathematics is not always explicit. An extension should provide a link between the Logo and the mathematics. It should allow the children to study mathematics, while retaining all the benefits of the Logo microworld which has been extended.

In practical terms this means that the software should provide a set of extra procedures which the children might regard as primitive. It should allow them to work at top-level, where they can write, edit and execute their own procedures as well as use those of the extension. Logo is an extensible language, and so extra procedures can be written to be used as though they were primitive to the language. But their use is not forced in any way. The procedures simply exist in the computer's workspace, and they can be called when they are needed. The user always has the full power of the Logo language available to her, and whatever the extension provides is additional to that power. The software should neither ask explicit questions, as might occur in more conventional computer-assisted learning, nor provide a menu of commands from which the user is forced to choose. There should be no structured activity built into its design.

Thus an extension should only constrain children's thinking in positive ways. It should emphasise some particular mathematical concept, or area of study, by providing a new environment for the children to explore. This environment may be more clearly defined than the one in which they are used to working, but the children must not feel that the actions are limited.

In the remainder of this chapter we will describe four further mathematical extensions, of which Several Turtles and Grids can be obtained through the ATM Logo Group.

Three dimensions

This software[6] allows the children to imagine that the turtle is moving in space, and the drawings on the monitor screen are all in perspective. FD, BK, LT and RT are used as normal in the plane of the turtle, and two new commands ROLL and PITCH turn the turtle into different planes.

Some sort of physical model is essential for the child. In two dimensions the child can use a floor turtle, or she can play turtle herself. When she uses the screen turtle she can refer to these concrete models mentally whenever she needs to. In 3D children might be introduced to the two new sorts of turn through paper aeroplanes. There is the slight disadvantage that real aeroplanes roll in order to turn left or right whereas in 3D Logo these movements are independent. Another possibility is for the children to play turtle on the wall bars in the gymnasium. In this case our inability to fly might be a more serious drawback. However, it does prove to be difficult for children to understand the turtle's path in three dimensions, and the result on the screen is not always what was expected, so the need for a physical model is paramount.

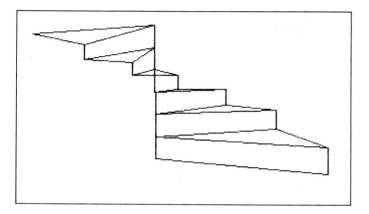

FIGURE 8.5   A staircase drawn with the 3D software

The staircase shown in Fig. 8.5 is an example of the use of the 3D software. Horatio Regini, the originator of 3D, provided the code for the staircase in an edition of *Micromath*[7].

Several turtles

Another extension which we have used with reasonable success is called TURTLES. This allows the children to create any number of turtles on the screen. The important extra procedures are TELL, to indicate which turtle is being addressed, FACE, to instruct one turtle to point towards another, and CRASH?, to detect whether a turtle is in the immediate vicinity of another. The two main types of activity which the TURTLES software motivates are races and curves of pursuit. Most of the races which the children designed used two turtles, with a recursive procedure to move them forward through random distances:

```
TO RACE
   TELL 1
   FD RANDOM 10
   TELL 2
   FD RANDOM 10
END
```

The curves of pursuit were often similar, with one procedure to set the turtles at the correct starting position and another recursive procedure to make them move:

```
TO CHASE
   TELL 1
   FD 10
   TELL 2
   FACE 1
   FD 10
   CHASE
END
```

Some of the children were able to write a line such as IF CRASH? 2 [STOP] to go after the first TELL 1 command. (David amended his version so that the direction of one of the turtles was controlled with two keys, and the other turtle chased it. The aim was to avoid a crash, which caused the screen to flash and the game to end.)

Unlike sprites, these simulated turtles have no speed, and they cannot assume different shapes. There is really only one turtle, and on using TELL it moves across the screen and adopts a different identity. This process is fairly slow, but the advantage of TURTLES is that the software is not expensive. Sprites may not be available for your machines, and if they are the extra hardware you need may cost more than the Logo. Any handbook to go with TURTLES would echo the sentiments of the DART handbook, and stress that the software could be valuable, but if the real thing becomes available TURTLES should be thrown away.

Grids

The facility to place grids of various types on the screen is one which may be valuable at an early stage. Many children challenge themselves to draw three-dimensional pictures long before they are ready to grapple with the 3D microworld described above. A realistic alternative would be to type ISOGRID 50 in order to display an isometric grid of dots, with each dot 50 units apart. The children can then manoeuvre the turtle in the usual way, but restricting themselves to movements of 50 or multiples of 50, and turns of 60°, 120° or 180°. In this way the turtle will always be positioned at one of the dots on the screen, and the children will be supported in their attempts to draw three-dimensional pictures (Fig. 8.6). At the end, the dots may be removed by typing NOISOGRID 50.

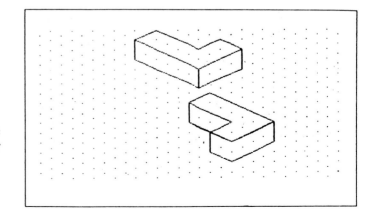

FIGURE 8.6   A grid produced with the ISOGRID procedure to help in the drawing of three-dimensional representations

Other children may want to create patterns which are based on a square grid, and so the commands SQGRID and

NOSQGRID are also available. In fact there is no reason why a variety of grids should not become part of the file, and many teachers will be able to add their own favourites.

Newton

To end this chapter we will describe a newtonian microworld which allows children to simulate forces and to observe the behaviour of the masses to which they are applied. This software is an extension to the microworld of sprites, and it is available from GEM Software[8] for the RML Nimbus computer which has sprites built into the Logo. The software was written for sixth-formers who are studying newtonian mechanics, but it is not inappropriate to use it with younger children too. As in other microworlds, the concepts are not forced in any way, but they are there to be learned as the children explore.

One of the simplest ideas to explore is the effect of gravity. SETMASS 1 sets the mass of the sprite, and SETFORCE 10 180 means that a force of 10 will be applied in a downward direction. Typing FOREVER [FORCE] makes the sprite move faster and faster towards the bottom of the screen. If the shape of the sprite is made into a circle, these commands will simulate a ball which has been dropped. The student may want to throw the ball, rather than dropping it.

```
TO THROW
  SETSPEED 0
  SETPOS [−140 −90]
  SETDIR 30
  SETSPEED 50 FOREVER [FORCE]
END
```

The path of the ball will now be a parabola starting near the bottom left-hand corner of the screen. An appropriate challenge at this stage might be to find out the maximum range of the ball when it is thrown at a particular speed from ground level. The idea can be extended by considering the effect of throwing the ball from the top of a cliff. There are many projects which can be developed using this theme. For instance, a program could be written for an archery contest. There might be some random element in the initial speed and direction of the arrow, and then points would be allocated according to where the arrow hit the target.

Inclined planes and flowing rivers provide further possibilities. To simulate the path of a sliding object, three forces need to be applied: gravity, friction and a reaction from the plane. An appropriate challenge would be to get the object to move at a constant speed. Gravity is not of any consequence in a river (provided that you can swim, that is). Here the problem is to determine the direction in which to swim so that you reach the other bank directly opposite the point where you left the first bank.

9   Afterword

For many teachers and many schools, the previous chapter is irrelevant. The extensions which were described often assume that the children are already very familiar with Logo. We have included it because some teachers do need to find ways to extend the children's activities, but it would be dangerous to suggest that the future must lie in this direction. By the time your children have exhausted the possibilities of turtle graphics, there may be new and better languages for use in school.

In our view Logo is the best language which is available now. Some teachers argue that children should learn more than one language. After all, experienced programmers use different tools for different jobs. But the children are learning, and so they need to be provided with one consistent environment in which to work. A rally driver may be able to drive off in any car, but the learner driver needs to practice in the car she knows.

We hope that we have made it perfectly clear throughout this book that Logo is valuable because of the educational philosophy that can go with it. If teachers can achieve similar results with other languages, or without computers, all well and good. Conversely, if Logo is taught formally, with all the children learning about REPEAT and then practising the new technique, it may not be worth the effort in the first place.

While we have no regrets about ignoring other programming languages, we are sorry not to have used spreadsheets or any of the other exciting software which is developing so quickly. In our classes the computers were used exclusively for Logo. Unfortunately the number of hours in the day is limited, and so is the number of computers in a school, and it does take plenty of time to reap the benefits of a Logo environment. All teachers will have to find the right balance for themselves in this respect. While no solution can be entirely satisfactory, do be aware of the dangers of spreading scarce resources too thinly and not doing justice to anything.

The main consideration at all times should be whether the children are in control of what they are learning. If you have reached this stage of the book, you probably have some commitment to Logo, but it is still not inappropriate to finish with this quotation from Seymour Papert's book *Mindstorms*:

'In many schools today, the phrase "computer-aided instruction" means making the computer teach the child. One might say the *computer is being used to program* the child. In my vision, *the child programs the computer . . .*'

References

Introduction

1 *Mindstorms — Children, Computers and Powerful Ideas*, ISBN 0-71080-472-5, by Seymour Papert, can be obtained from:

Harvester Press Ltd.
16 Ship Street
Brighton
Sussex

Chapter 2

1 RML Logo is the only full version of Logo which is available for the 380Z and 480Z machines. RML also produce their own Logo for the Nimbus. For further information contact:

Research Machines Ltd.
Post Office Box 75
Mill Street
Oxford OX2 0BW
Telephone number: 0865 249866

2 Logotron Logo is the most popular version of Logo for the BBC computer. It is a standard LCSI version available on a chip. For further information contact:

Logotron Ltd.
Dales Brewery
Gwydir Street
Cambridge CB1 2LS
Telephone number: 0223 323656

Chapter 3

1 The most popular floor turtles are the Valiant Turtle, which is remote controlled, and the Jessop Turtle, which may be remote controlled or connected by a cable. For further information contact:

Valiant Technology Ltd.
Gulf House
370 York Road
London SW18 1SP
Telephone number: 01 874 8747

Jessop–Ralph Ltd.
Unit 5
7 Long Street
London E2 8HN
Telephone number: 01 739 3232

2 We have not seen them used in the classroom, but successors to George are available through toyshops, and they are manufactured by:

Systema A (UK) Ltd.
12 Albury Close
Loverock Road
Reading RG3 1BB
Telephone number: 0734 502223/586429

3 DART is a turtle graphics package for the BBC computer. It is available from:

Advisory Unit
Endymion Road
Hatfield
Hertfordshire
Telephone number: 07072 65443

4 ARROW is a turtle graphics package for RML computers (380Z, 480Z and NIMBUS). It is available from:

Computer Education Unit
Wheatley Centre
Littleworth Road
Wheatley
Oxfordshire
Telephone number: 08677 3980

Chapter 6

1 *Mathematics Counts*, Report of the Committee of Inquiry into the Teaching of Mathematics in Schools, chaired by Dr. W. H. Cockcroft, is available from HMSO or through booksellers.

2 *Mathematics from 5 to 16*, Curriculum Matters 3, an HMI series, is available from HMSO or through booksellers.

3 *Points of Departure*, numbers 1 and 2 are available from:
Association of Teachers of Mathematics
7 Shaftesbury Street
Derby DE3 8YB
Telephone number: 0332 46599

4 *How to Solve It*, ISBN 0–691–02356–5, by George Polya, is published by:
Princeton University Press
Princeton, NJ
USA

5 *Generating Mathematical Activity in the Classroom*, by Marion Bird, is available from:

The Mathematics Centre
West Sussex Institute of Higher Education
Bognor Regis College
Upper Bognor Road
Bognor Regis
West Sussex PO21 1HR

Chapter 8

1 The CLARE (Control Logo and the Real Environment) package contains the CLARE board, software for the BBC, RML 380Z and 480Z computers, and documentation. It is available from:

Advisory Unit
Endymion Road
Hatfield
Hertfordshire
Telephone number: 07072 65443

2 The CONTROL LOGO software is for use with the BBC computer with Logotron Logo. It is available, with documentation, from:

Logotron Ltd.
Dales Brewery
Gwydir Street
Cambridge CB1 2LS
Telephone number: 0223 323656

3 The LOGOSOUNDS software is for use with the BBC computer with Logotron Logo. It is available, with documentation, from:

Advisory Unit
Endymion Road
Hatfield
Hertfordshire
Telephone number: 07072 65443

4 The LOGO MUSIC software is for use with the BBC computer with Logotron Logo. It is available, with documentation, from:

Logotron Ltd.
Dales Brewery
Gwydir Street
Cambridge CB1 2LS
Telephone number: 0223 323656

5 The ATM Logo Microworlds software is produced by the ATM Logo Working Group. It is available through:

Association of Teachers of Mathematics
7 Shaftesbury Street
Derby DE3 8YB
Telephone number: 0332 46599

6 The 3D Logo software is for use with the BBC computer with Logotron Logo. It is available, with documentation, from:

Logotron Ltd.
Dales Brewery
Gwydir Street
Cambridge CB1 2LS
Telephone number: 0223 323656

7 *Micromath* is a journal of the Association of Teachers of Mathematics. It is published three times a year, and non-members of the Association of Teachers of Mathematics can subscribe through:

Basil Blackwell Ltd.
108 Cowley Road
Oxford OX4 1JF
Telephone number: 0865 791100

8 GEM Software
58 Parklands Avenue
Lillington
Leamington Spa
Warwickshire
Telephone number: 0926 20800

Some useful books and resources

Teaching and Learning With Logo, ISBN 0-7099-3572-2, by Allan Martin, a book for teachers, is published by:

Croom Helm Ltd.
Provident House
Burrell Row
Beckenham
Kent BR3 1AT

Learning with Logo — Some Classroom Experiences, ISBN 0-86184-163-8, by Beverly Anderson, is available from:

Tecmedia
5 Granby Street
Loughborough
Leicestershire LE11 3DU

Microworlds — Adventures with Logo, ISBN 0-09-161111-3, by Richard Noss, Clare Smallman and Michael Thorne, a book for children, is published by:

Hutchinson and Co. Ltd.
17–21 Conway Street
London W1P 6JD

Mathematics and Logo Pack This pack contains pupil materials, posters and a teachers' guide. It is produced for lower-secondary school children, but it is appropriate for a wide range of ages. For further information contact:

SMILE Centre
Middle Row School

Kensal Row
London W10 5DB
Telephone number: 01 960 7330

Turning Point, a film about primary-aged children using Logo, is intended to accompany the in-service education pack of materials called *Posing and Solving Problems Using Logo*, produced by the MEP National Primary Project. It is available separately from:

Videotext Educational Publishing
Orders Department
Eagle Star House
New North Road
Exeter EX4 4HF
Telephone number: 0392 219309

Starting Point is a video intended to accompany the in-service education pack of materials called *Infant and First Schools — the Role of the Micro*, produced by the MEP National Primary Project. The video is available separately from:

Elston Bray Video Services
54 Crofton Road
London SE5 8NB
Telephone number: 01 701 0975

and

56 Cranleigh Drive
Swanley
Kent BR8 8NX
Telephone number: 0322 69660

Wondermaths — Logo: five 15-minute programmes for upper-primary children. For further information contact:

BBC Television
School Broadcasting Information
Villiers House
The Broadway
London W5 2PA
Telephone number: 01 991 8015

Index